Mary G. Durkin, wife and mother, is also the Director of the Northwest Suburban Learning Center, School for New Learning, DePaul University. She is also a teacher in the theology department at DePaul. Active in religious education for several years, she founded, in 1966, the Ladies' Theology Program in her parish which currently serves over 200 women.

The Suburban Woman

THE Suburban Woman

Her Changing Role in the Church

MARY G. DURKIN

A CROSSROAD BOOK
The Seabury Press · New York

250.2
D935

202955

The Seabury Press, Inc.
815 Second Avenue
New York, N.Y. 10017

Copyright © 1975 by Mary G. Durkin. All rights reserved. No part of this
book may be reproduced in any manner whatsoever, except for brief
quotations in critical reviews and articles, without written permission from
the publisher.

Printed in the United States of America

Library of Congress Cataloging in Publication Data

Durkin, Mary G   1934-
  The suburban woman.

  "A Crossroad book."
  Bibliography: p.
  1. Women in church work.   2. Women.   3. Sub-
urban life.   I. Title.
BV4415.D83   250   75-29147
ISBN 0-8164-1200-6

to Jack, a special suburban man

Contents

Preface

For a period of nine years I lived in two different worlds. I was a part-time student at the Divinity School of the University of Chicago and a full-time wife and mother in Park Ridge, a suburb some fifteen miles northwest of the Chicago Loop. In my travels between the two locations I had a great deal of time to consider the distance between the two worlds. It seems natural that I would reflect on the distance between the research and ideas being discussed in the divinity school and the day-to-day lives of the members of the suburban community.

Theologians are the Church's teachers; yet it is impossible to teach people unless one understands them. I found that there is a tendency for a theology faculty to become cut off from the problems of the general church membership. At the same time there is a fear on the part of many parishioners that the theologians are destroying the church. Such lack of communication is destructive for the church and all its members.

With this gap in mind I elected to do my doctoral dissertation on an approach to narrowing that gap for one segment of the suburban population: the women. Since I was most familiar with the situation of women this seemed the logical place to begin the work of translating the ideas of the university to the world of suburbia. I hope that I have also been able to make the university more aware of the suburban situation.

Obviously during my nine years of study many professors have contributed ideas which have found their way into this book. There are some, however, whom I would like to thank specifically for their support and encouragement. Mr. Joseph Sittler, Father David Tracy and Mr. Martin Marty have been steadfast supporters of the validity of this approach to the study of theology and their encouragement was most helpful. Mr. James Gustafson, who came to the school just as I was beginning the dissertation was extremely helpful in advising on the important points to include in the final thesis.

In addition to faculty support, there are many people who assisted me in writing the dissertation and in revising it for publication. I would like to acknowledge their help and thank them. Dr. Kathleen McCourt of the National Opinion Research Center was most gracious in advising me how to gather sociological material in in-depth interviews. The clergy of my parish—Mary, Seat of Wisdom—and the ten women who gave up their time to be interviewed were extremely cooperative in answering questions.

The revision of the dissertation into this book could not have taken place without the support and cooperation of many people. My colleagues at the School for New Learning were extremely encouraging during this time. Marilyn Stocker spent many hours helping me refine my position on some of the issues since the completion of the dissertation. Without the extraordinary cooperation of Dorothy Inserra the final copy for this book would not have been completed, and I wish to acknowledge my deep appreciation of her gift of time, often typing under pressure.

Finally there are those people who have been so much a part of my life that everything they do has undoubtedly had an impact on the work I have done. To my sibling, Andrew Greeley, who has supported and encouraged me at every point I wish to express my thanks for being a "pushy Irish Priest" when I needed it most. To Laura, Julie, Eileen, Sean, Dan, Anne, and Elizabeth my thanks and the hope that others will find them as interesting and enjoyable as I do. To Jack for helping me escape the mythical world of the suburban woman and for being a partner with me in enjoying the real world, a thank-you hardly seems adequate; but it would take another book to explain his role in helping me work through the issues I am addressing here.

1
Introduction

As a young housewife I had never envisioned myself as an organizer of anything more complex than infant feeding and bathing schedules. For this reason, whenever someone introduces me as the founder of the Ladies' Theology Program I am moved to reflect that the Spirit often uses unknowing agents. In the winter of 1966 when I gathered with thirty other suburban housewives for the first semester of what has developed into a highly successful program of theological education for women, I could not have anticipated that nine years later the program would continue as a forum serving over two hundred women a semester. Nor could I have imagined that a group identifying itself as Theology West, located in a suburb fifteen miles west of us, would form in the fall of 1974 and attract an additional two hundred participants.

The growth and spread of the program are due to the efforts of many women who have actively participated over the years, but the initial session was my attempt to share some of the ideas I was being exposed to in my first year of study at the Divinity School of the

University of Chicago. Many friends had expressed the desire to do something similar, but lacking transportation (the University of Chicago is a twenty-five mile drive from suburban Park Ridge) and babysitters, they were unable to join me in formal course work. The logical response to their interest was to bring the teachers to them at a convenient time and place while providing a babysitting service.

Part of our pleasure at the small, but encouraging response to the first offering was undoubtedly a reaction to the skepticism of many toward our plans. The pastor of our parish had given his approval to the program with the warning that we probably would not find anyone willing to teach it nor anyone interested in attending. Needless to say, such advice only spurred us on to try harder. The participation in the program has attested to the validity of my initial proposal. It has also been a vindication of the enthusiasm of those who helped in the original planning of the program.

This experience was the beginning of my awareness of the particular dilemma of the suburban woman. My own involvement with the program, actively for a period of four years and as an observer for an additional five, coupled with my role as director of the suburban center of an adult college, has increased this awareness. Though it might appear that the suburban housewife remains complacent and aloof in the midst of the controversy surrounding the role of women in our society, an investigation into the lives of many of them indicates their considerable frustration.

Beleaguered administrators in academic, business, political and religious institutions, challenged by equal-rights advocates, might wish that all women were as content as the suburban housewife seems to be in her various roles as wife, mother, clubwoman, and church member. They often fail to perceive the signs of discontent displayed by the "little woman" in the home. As one successful lawyer friend remarked about his wife, an extremely bright and competent college graduate, "My wife is perfectly happy being involved in mothers' clubs. She moves right along with the kids from grammar school to high school, and I'm sure she'll find a mothers' club at whatever college they attend." While his assumption may be correct, it is obvious from his statement that he would have difficulty recognizing any disenchantment which might arise over time.

Feminists devote little attention to the needs of the suburban homemaker since she seems a disinterested bystander to their struggle for equality. While most of the suburban women I talk with agree that women should receive equal pay for equal work, they are not seriously considering careers and have not bothered to join the crusade for the Equal Rights Amendment. Also, most of them have no need for or desire to use free day-care centers, so a reduction of funds for such programs is not apt to stir them to action.

It is difficult for most suburban women who are happy with their commitment to marriage and motherhood to identify with the rhetoric of the radicals within the women's movement. However, as is evidenced by the increasing number of women who are returning to school "to prepare for being forty," there is a growing recognition on the part of many housewives of the need for some changes in their lifestyles. Due to the lack of attention to the problems of the suburban woman, their signals of dissatisfaction are often not understood by themselves or by those with whom they are involved. The frustrated suburban woman often feels singularly affected and doesn't know where to turn for support or advice. Most of the women I talked with, as well as those who come for educational counseling, feel they must work things out on their own.

Among those often unaware of the needs of the suburban woman is her parish priest or minister. Pastors tend to see suburban housewives only as wives, mothers, and church helpers. A pastor who describes the women of his parish as lovely, charming women who are dedicated to their families and willing to do any task as long as it is beneficial to the church community might be surprised by the comments of one of his parishioners. She maintains, "The priests simply are not aware of the great store of talent available among the women of this community. I am a qualified speech therapist, but the only thing I'm ever asked to do is help prepare for a fund-raising dinner."

Equally misguided in his approach to ministry to these women is the cleric who has succumbed to the party line of radical feminism. A group of ministerial students at the University of Chicago expressed disbelief when I told them that the name of our program was Ladies' Theology. They were convinced that in this day no group with the label *ladies* could possibly be dedicated to serious study. They were also sure that no aware woman would want to be labeled a lady, given the negative connotations associated with this title by the women's movement. When I asked the women about their reaction to the name of the program most were concerned that *theology* might frighten some less confident women. All but one saw nothing wrong with the term *ladies*. As one woman observed, "That's what we are, so why should it bother us?" Obviously one of these ministerial students would have difficulty understanding and ministering to a similar group of women.

Although the former approach is generally more acceptable (or less offensive) to the suburban woman, neither indicates a real awareness of her situation. The minister most often sees his role as one of counselor to those who come to him with their problems. For this task he considers it important to be well versed in the social sciences and to be trained in counseling skills that will be useful in crisis situations. He seldom addresses himself to a theological consideration of the woman's role.

There is increasing evidence that many priests and ministers working at the level of the local church are distrustful of theology. A local Lutheran minister who lists reading as one of his hobbies admits that he has not read a theology book in the two years since his ordination. A deacon serving in a parish church the year previous to his ordination to the priesthood returned to the seminary saying he had never had occasion to use his theology training. These are just two of the many indications that the task of pastoral theology is in need of serious review.

However, any cleric would be hard pressed to find much in textbook theology which would aid his ministry to the suburban woman. As the salesman at the local religious bookstore puts it: "There is very little available between the submissive woman of Marabel Morgan and the radical feminist of Mary Daly."

The Total Woman, Marabel Morgan's bestseller,[1] though claiming to be based on the scriptural definition of woman's role, could hardly be considered a pastoral theology for women. However, the course that accompanies the book, as well as one entitled *Fascinating Womanhood*,[2] are being offered at an increasing number of Protestant churches. These courses appeal to the desire of the suburban woman to be a perfect wife and mother, though they leave little room for her to develop as an individual.

On the other hand, Mary Daly's *Beyond God the Father*,[3] with its emphasis on the need for women to overcome the oppression of the patriarchal society, leaves the woman with little opportunity to enjoy her role as wife and mother. Also, as part of the radical feminist movement, it fails to take into consideration any diversity among women. This approach is often used to make all males feel responsible for the oppression of women and all women feel guilty if they are not fighting for liberation.

It is not surprising that there is a lack of guidelines on a pastoral theology for the suburban women. The suburban woman has two strikes against her: first of all, she is a woman. The majority of theologians are men who, at this stage of our cultural development, find it extremely difficult to understand women. To develop a theological position on women would be virtually impossible for most of them. The few women who are engaged in theological discourse have, in many instances, been subjected to specific oppressions, and are addressing their work to that aspect of the woman's issue.

The second disadvantage for the suburban woman is that she is a suburbanite. There is, in addition to a large degree of male chauvinism in theology faculties, a certain cynicism concerning suburbia. During my days as a student I often heard middle-class suburbia referred to as a vast cultural and intellectual wasteland. This same attitude seemed prevalent among the clergy in the 1960s. Fortunately there now appears to be a shift to an appreciation of the challenge of ministry in suburban churches.

What is still lacking, however, is the recognition that the role of church leader or pastor carries with it a responsibility to articulate a theological vision which will awaken a response from the members of the community. It is the task of pastoral theology to develop such a vision.

Leaders of local churches must develop a theology which will meet the needs of the suburban woman. The local churches must point to ways that the suburban housewife can live her multidimensional life in a manner which will be rewarding to her and her family —and be a sign to the community of the goodness and love of God.

Given the suburban woman's need for help in confronting the dilemma of her situation, and the obvious lack of serious attention to this situation by national church leaders and theologians, it is incumbent on local church ministers and lay leaders to devote their attention to the problem. Following the advice of Bernard Lonergan on the principles of subsidiarity which require that "at the local levels problems will be defined and, insofar as possible, worked out,"[4] this book will begin to develop a pastoral theology of and for the suburban woman. It will seek to define the experience in the local church and propose solutions to the problem. If such solutions can be implemented at the local level it is possible that we will begin to fill the gap between Marabel Morgan and Mary Daly.

Before presenting this approach to a pastoral theology of women, it is important to clarify what I mean by pastoral theology. This should serve as a basis for understanding my proposal that others, both laity and clergy, join me in exploring various ways of implementing this approach in local churches.

Pastoral theology, at the local level, in both Catholic and Protestant churches, has always consisted of instructions for clerical behavior, providing norms, regulations and pastoral experiences which would guide the leader of the community in carrying out the duties of his apostolate.[5] Protestant emphasis has been on better ways of preaching the Word, while Catholic pastoral theology was primarily an implementation of moral theology.

As both religious traditions became aware of the need to be relevant in the contemporary world, there was a sharp shift in emphasis concerning the key dimensions of ministry. This shift occurred on a grand scale in the Catholic Church at the time of the Second Vatican Council. Priests who had come to rely on manuals of moral and pastoral theology experienced a great void. Seminaries quickly filled that void for their students with courses in social science, counseling and group dynamics, so we now have young priests supposedly equipped for their pastoral role in a more democratic parish structure. According to H. Richard Niebuhr a somewhat earlier shift in Protestantism caused mass confusion regarding the aim of theological education. Many aspiring ministers found less emphasis on theology in their seminary training.[6]

Although one can find little fault with the aims of the churches to be relevant, I am dismayed with their failure to realize that relevance for a Christian church must flow from a grasp of what it is which makes the Church a unique component of the culture. It is a rude awakening for many priests and ministers when they suddenly begin to question what it is they are doing in their clerical role that could not be performed as well, if not better, by someone outside the Church.

It is not just the function of the ordained ministry within the churches which must be understood from a theological perspective. The entire church community must recognize that, without its theological dimension, it is just another social group. This recovery of an understanding of the theological dimension of the Christian churches is mandatory for the development of a pastoral theology of women which will challenge and support them as they begin to consider future lifestyles.

The necessity of a theological component in the Church's approach to clarifying the experience of women requires that our pastoral theology be both an art and a science. The method of pastoral theology which I am using is based on a program of pastoral theology developed by John Shea, a Catholic theologian who served as a parish priest prior to teaching theology at the seminary in Chicago. According to Shea, pastoral theology is an art:

> In a very real sense the pastoral theologian is analogous to the artist. Through his skill he helps to create a consciousness in a community of its meaning and responsibility. He is called to be in Nietzsche's words "poet to our everyday lives." This reference to poetry brings out the pre-cognitive feel for the religious dimension of life that characterizes great pastoral theology . . . as a pastoral theologian the minister engages in, for himself and the community, the primordial act of interpreting the Really Real and trying to live in communion with it. This is a fundamental drive which, when exercised in the concrete, draws on the most creative aspects of the human personality.[7]

A practitioner of this art of pastoral theology must be well versed in the science of pastoral or practical theology.[8] It is possible to be a pastoral theologian in the manner Shea presents only if one is aware of the cognitive meaning of the Christian message. Shea developed his approach to pastoral theology in an attempt to help the pastoral minister and, specifically, the Catholic priest, overcome his identity crisis. The method he proposes could also be implemented by concerned lay church members.

This book is an adaptation of the three elements of Shea's method of pastoral theology to the situation of the suburban woman. Further, it will attempt to identify ways in which clergy and lay people might work together, exercising the most creative aspects of their personalities and arriving at a common consciousness of the meaning and responsibility of the Christian community.

The first stage in this approach to pastoral theology is to identify and elaborate the paradigmatic experiences of an individual or group. To do this, Shea maintains we must listen not just to what the women are saying about themselves, but we must listen at a much deeper level. We must be able to discern the common religious needs and experiences of these women, even before they are completely aware of their existence. By examining her cultural background, which was influential in forming the suburban woman's self-image, and investigating her present lifestyle, we will listen for those key experiences which have formed and shaped her.

Once we have named and explored these key experiences, we will use the Christian tradition to illuminate and direct these experiences. It is at this point that familiarity with the science of pastoral theology, which is the final stage of systematic theological reflection, is required. The pastoral theologian must have extensive knowledge of the Christian tradition, being able to place an experience in the framework of the Christian world view. Placing the experience of the suburban woman within the framework of her membership in a local church will give it a perspective and focus which have not been considered previously.

Finally, we must develop a strategy of action that flows from the self-understanding achieved through the merging of the experience of the suburban woman and the tradition of membership in a local church. This final stage is the most difficult one, given the vast polarization in all the churches concerning the role of women. It will be important to bear in mind Shea's caution that "there is *no one* Christian response to each personal and political problem. . . . Our response is Christian as long as it emerges from a Christian style. It is non-Christian insofar as it contradicts that style."[9]

The strategies of action which I propose will be a first step in a continuing investigation of the role of the responsible Christian woman. This investigation is necessary for me as I encounter new opportunities for growth in my own life. If the sharing of my ideas will be of benefit to others, I will be pleased. I also hope that their response to my proposals will provide me with new insights.

My primary insight comes from my own experience as a suburban woman over the past eighteen years. For the last nine years I have been closely involved with other women in a variety of projects over and above the normal "neighboring" of a suburban community, and it is from these experiences that I gleaned most of my sense of what constitutes our paradigmatic experience.

The Ladies' Theology Program, which I refer to throughout this book, is a daytime adult education program for women in the Chicago suburb of Park Ridge, Illinois. It was my experience with this program that led to my eventual doctoral work on the topic of a pastoral theology for and of suburban women. For my dissertation, I interviewed ten women who had been or were currently participating in the program. In these in-depth interviews I tried to determine the women's positions on a variety of issues related to their self-image, their relationship with the church, and their general views on issues important in their lives and in the world. I also interviewed four of the clergy from the parish where the program began, questioning them on their views of the program, of the women in their community, and on their theological vision of a parish. Much of the material I gathered in the course of these interviews is contained in this book.

For the past two years I have been actively involved with the School for New Learning, a new, non-traditional college of DePaul University. The college offers adult learners the opportunity to design their own education and to obtain credit for life experience gained outside formal schooling.

For eighteen months I have served as director of an external learning center of the School, located in Park Ridge. In my role as director of the center, I have had the opportunity to work with many suburban women who either have returned to school or are considering that possibility. I have also taught courses for the School in the suburban setting, one course specially designed for women. This experience with the School has supplied me with additional insights into the situation of the suburban woman, while at the same time re-enforcing some of my earlier hypotheses arrived at during my involvement with the smaller group of women in the theology program.

I am applying this technique of listening to these women, just as Shea is directing the pastoral theologian to listen. Although this is obviously only one narrow segment of the population, it is essential that this group of middle-class women also be considered in the churches' attempts to fulfill their mission of witnessing to the message of Jesus.

2
The Mythical World of the Suburban Woman

Undoubtedly, many of the female readers of this book have found themselves confronted with the demand of a male friend, co-worker or even a husband to, "Tell me, what is it you women want, anyway?" Such a demand is often followed with comments concerning the many advantages the suburban woman has which the male wishes he could enjoy. After all, look at all the time the housewife has for sleeping late, shopping, playing tennis, kaffee-klatching, etc. Or some male manager will complain that "We treat our women here very well. In fact with the affirmative action laws and the government breathing down our necks, we're anxious to promote qualified women. But most of the women refuse to aspire to a higher job."

There is, of course, no simple answer to this complex question. Women are not sure what they want and often disagree among themselves on their aspirations. The variety of responses to the Equal Rights Amendment demonstrates that there is no one "woman's" demand.

While I generally suggest to my male questioner that it is unreasonable to expect all women to want the same thing—any more than all men—inwardly I find myself mulling over the behavior of various suburban women and wondering why a suburban housewife with a master's degree in guidance and counseling is perfectly content to stay home and care for her home and two school-age children while a forty-five year old mother of nine is working as a part-time medical social worker and taking courses toward the completion of her bachelor's degree? I can't explain why an extremely talented woman who engaged in highly creative and challenging volunteer work in the field of marriage education takes a clerical job using none of her talents and says: "It's just fine for me. I put in my hours. They give me a nice check and I don't have to travel far from home."

What explanation exists for the personal difficulties talented and capable women experience when they move up to a higher position in their work situation? As the female affirmative action manager for a large corporation remarked: "There are lots of talented housewives who have come to work for us in the past few years. Many of them are better educated than their supervisors. But they look at the frustrations of the women managers around here and decide they don't want to chance a managerial role."

And why is it that suburban housewives in their late thirties and early forties, who claim they want to return to school, are incapable of defining educational goals for themselves? They come to our program eagerly anticipating that we will give them a goal and steer them to the perfect career.

Although I know the answers to all these questions are not simple, I believe we must try to find causes for the actions of today's women. Only then will we begin to have some insight into the experience of the suburban woman. To identify the paradigmatic experience of this group, we must deal with the complexity of their situation. We must be willing to listen with open minds to hints about their hopes and their fears. We must recognize the conflict in their lives, a conflict between the life goals they set for themselves some twenty or thirty years ago and the reality of their world today.

This investigation of the recent history of the woman's role is undertaken, not in order to blame anyone, but to try to understand the turmoil which we experience when we are confronted with drastic changes in our own and others' expectations of our role.

It is not necessary to penetrate too far beneath the surface to find the underlying causes for the dilemma. Those of us educated in the late forties, the fifties, and even the early sixties were taught that a woman's place is in the home and that her fulfillment in life comes from the satisfaction she experiences in the accomplishments of her husband and children. At the same time we live in a technologically affluent culture which no longer requires that we spend the major portion of our lives attending to the physical needs of our families. We also live longer, with a higher portion of our life span to be lived after our children have left the home.

During our developmental years, it appeared that the myth of Adam and Eve had been slightly revised. When God expelled this original couple from the Garden he commanded Adam to work by the sweat of his brow, but he promised that some day salvation would come and Adam would be allowed to move to middle-class suburbia. There, as a commuting husband and father, he would be head of his family. At the same time, he would resume his rightful position in man's world. At the time that Eve was ordered to bear her children in sorrow she was assured that some day she would be allowed to find her rightful place in her suburban middle-class home. There she would be the heart of the family and a support to Adam when he would need harbor from his trying struggles with the problems of the world. She would be an inspiration to her children, experiencing through their achievements the simple pleasures which fulfill a woman.

Examples of the strength of this cultural myth which developed great force in the post-World War II move-to-the-suburbs era, are found in such diverse places as the pages of women's magazines, the directives of papal pronouncements, the news and editorials of college newspapers, guides for women's Bible study groups and directives for couples preparing for marriage. "It's a man's world. Woman's place is in the home," expresses the whole set of attitudes concerning women which were prevalent when most of us who are suburban wives and mothers were attending school and beginning our marriages.

In *The Feminine Mystique,* Betty Friedan traces the emergence of the "Happy Housewife Heroine" in the pages of the women's magazines from the late forties to the beginning of the 1960s. Coinciding with the return of the fighting men to the work force and a large number of Rosie the Riveters to their homes, the women's magazines began to emphasize the theme of "togetherness" coined by *McCall's.* This togetherness, however, was not a togetherness where men and women worked side by side in solving the problems of the world. Rather, it was one which aimed at establishing a togetherness in the home with women's world "confined to her own body and beauty, the charming of man, husband, children and home."[1]

Both feature articles and fiction portrayed fulfillment for woman only in her home as housewife and
mother. *McCall's, Redbook* and *Ladies' Home Journal* all
emphasized woman in terms of her sexual role and
concentrated on those problems which might disturb
her adjustment as a housewife and her fulfillment as a
mother.

As a high school and college student, reading my
mother's copies of *McCall's* and *Ladies' Home Journal,*
and as a young married woman reading *Redbook,* I was
kept informed on such topics as:

"Feminity Begins at Home"; "It's a Man's World Maybe";
"Have Babies While You're Young"; "How to Snare a
Male"; "Should I Stop Working When We Marry?"; "Are
You Training Your Daughter to Be a Wife?"; "Do Women
Talk Too Much?"; "Really a Man's World, Politics"; "How
to Hold onto a Happy Marriage"; "Don't Be Afraid to
Marry Young"; "Cooking to Me Is Poetry"; "The Business
of Running a Home."

As a Catholic these articles reinforced my acceptance
of the Church's emphasis on the importance of motherhood and the role of woman as the heart of the home.
This was the era when "the best Catholic family was the
largest Catholic family," and, since suburban Catholic
women continued to have babies at a much later age
than their non-Catholic contemporaries, we could anti-
cipate a considerable number of extra years in which
motherhood would be a full-time occupation. Our non-
Catholic peers did not, however, devote less time to
motherhood. They just had more time to spend on
each child.

Much of the Catholic Church's instructional emphasis during this period viewed the primary (and for
some educators, the only) purpose of marriage as the
procreation and education of children. An examina-

tion of the image of woman presented in various segments of Catholic culture helps in our understanding of the attitudes we acquired concerning our role. A similar look at several views within Protestant teaching from the same era will indicate that religious differences on some topics did not carry over to the image of women.

The official pronouncements of the Catholic Church expressed by Pope Pius XII (1939–1958), although encouraging women to be active in apostolic works, reflect a certain contradiction when they turn to discussing the role of wife and mother.

When speaking to a group of Italian women, the pope proclaimed that the Creator has fashioned woman, her organism and her spirit for motherhood. This is why she experiences fear when the social or political order threatens her vocation as a mother. The world is awakening with alarm to the realization of the results of a loss of respect for the woman's place of honor in the home as housewife and mother.

He warned of the dire consequences of the mother being absent from the home. Family life offers no attraction to the children when the homes become desolate for lack of care and when family members, working in different parts of the city, hardly have time to spend together. The children's education, and especially that of the daughter, suffers when the mother is not present as an example of training for real life. The daughter will not be inclined to the austerities of housework and will fail to appreciate its dignity and beauty. The daughter of the well-to-do who sees all the household chores done by hired help, while the mother engages in frivolous occupations and futile amusements, will have no desire to devote herself to the home as a wife and mother. She will want only to live her own life.[2]

In his various statements during this period, the pontiff made frequent reference to the essential difference between men and women. Although the dignity of woman is acknowledged as a God-given right which has been upheld throughout the ages by the Church, this dignity was seen as deriving from those qualities in her which are complementary to those of man. This has been ordained by the Creator for the essential mission of woman, which is motherhood.

In an address to newlyweds, the pope warned brides of the evils of the day: those which introduced opportunities for women to engage in activities similar to those of men and even allowed some husbands and wives to find themselves in positions of equality. This is contrary to the Christian concept of marriage in which wives should be subject to their husbands as the Church is subject to Christ. The young bride was cautioned: "Do not react like Eve to these lying, tempting deceitful voices." Instead she should: "accept . . . this authority of your husbands, to whom God has subjected you according to the dispositions of nature and grace; . . . and love it with the same respectful love you bear towards the authority of Our Lord Himself."

Needless to say, most American girls who were growing up during these years did not hear these papal pronouncements so directly. Their message, however, was contained in much of the instruction we received from the clergy and nuns. Marriage talks in high school and college, plus the series of instructions which couples preparing for marriage received from the parish priest, all followed the basic theme on woman's role expressed by the pope.

The literature and philosophy of the Cana movement during our formative years is an excellent example of how a view of woman's place developed in the mind of the Catholic girl who eventually became a suburban housewife. The Cana Conference, a movement dedicated to the task of marriage education, began in the Archdiocese of Chicago in the early 1940s. Its original purpose was to provide married couples with insights into the marital relationship, in an attempt to stem the rising tide of divorce. When it became apparent that premarital counseling was an important aid to marital success, the Pre-Cana branch of the movement developed.

By the mid-1950s most couples wishing to be married in the Chicago archdiocese were required first to attend a Pre-Cana Conference. Here they heard talks by a priest, a married couple, and a physician on the spiritual, practical, and physical aspects of marriage, thus relieving the parish priest of the task of sexual instruction.

Cana and Pre-Cana conferences were well received in the Chicago area from the late forties until the mid-sixties. Couples welcomed the opportunity to discuss their concerns and hear experts in the field of marriage. The success of the Chicago Cana Conference made it a model for the rest of the country.

The Cana "party line" on woman's role was absorbed by large numbers of Catholic women during these years. As a young woman marrying in the mid-1950s, I had been exposed to the Cana message in a series of talks at my high school, in my college marriage course taught by a Cana priest, at a special Lenten Forum for young adults conducted by a Cana team, at a Pre-Cana conference and at a Cana conference a few years after my marriage. And my experience was typical of that of many of my peers.

A study of the reactions by most couples to the three central themes of Cana on this topic reveals, however, that some of this acceptance was in response to the general emphasis of the culture of the time and not entirely in obedience to a unique Catholic position. These themes were: (1) Man is the head, woman is the heart; (2) Men and women are psychologically as well as physically different; and, (3) Working wives cause problems for a marriage.

Most couples went along with the first two themes, but the third was not as enthusiastically accepted. After all, the second income of the new bride would go a long way towards the down payment on the house in the suburbs which the couple planned to buy within the first few years of marriage. By the mid-fifties the Cana speakers relented somewhat on this position. While still maintaining that the ideal situation was one in which the wife would not work, some concessions were made to reality. Couples were warned not to use both incomes for living expenses, or they might be tempted to postpone having children rather than give up a lifestyle which could not continue once the wife stopped working. Only the most dire circumstances would allow a woman to return to work after the birth of her first child. From that point on, the husband was to be the sole support of the family.

This latter point was readily accepted by participants in the various Cana programs. When my husband and I served as host couple at Pre-Cana conferences we would hear repeated testimony of the traumas which occurred when a mother worked. As I look back on those testimonials I am struck by the fact that most of them came from the men in the group. This was not an indication that the women favored working after they had children. The majority did not. They were eager to devote themselves to the role of wife and mother, and considered this a full-time job. Their intended spouses did not have to worry about them wanting to return to a job. Indeed, many were bored with their jobs and anxious to begin a family in order to escape from a dull work situation.

Most young women in those days were not career oriented. Those who attended college did so with the dual purpose of supporting themselves until they married and finding a husband. Career choices open to women were limited in those days. As a friend of mine who dropped out of college after the second year remarked recently, "The only reason to stay in school then was to become a nurse or a teacher, and I didn't want to be either of those. So I quit and became a secretary. What I really wanted was to be an artist, but my family didn't see what good that would do me in marriage." She expressed a great deal of envy of young college women in the 1970s who have much wider career options.

Interestingly, of the women I interviewed only four mentioned marriage as one of their goals during their high school years. However, the others did indicate that their high school career dream was only to fill the time prior to marriage. High school ambitions mentioned, but never followed through on, were teacher, nurse, medical technologist, actress, journalist, and lawyer. One woman who was most emphatic in her response to the question concerning her life goals while in high school "wanted to be a psychologist and travel, travel, travel; I didn't want to marry until I was at least twenty-five." She married at twenty and had five children in seven years. Another who, while in high school, wanted "to be a teacher, get married and have a family," did just that. For the rest, the commitment that most careers other than teaching, required led them to settle for less involved—and often less interesting—jobs.

My own high school dream of being an actress had been replaced in early college years with becoming a social worker. However, when I became engaged at the end of my junior year, I changed to education courses which would allow me to teach. I considered that the ideal job, since as a working bride I would be home early and have sufficient time to prepare dinner for my husband. Teaching was also a good insurance policy in the event that some dire circumstances did arise. A teacher's hours would coincide with my children's school schedule.

It really did not matter that while I was a working bride, my husband was attending college and working and never arrived home until midnight to eat what I prepared for him. Nor did it matter to me at the time that I was not particularly enthusiastic about teaching, since I never envisioned any of these dire circumstances arising. I planned to work only until I had my first child, which I hoped would be within a year after our marriage.

What did matter for those of us attending college in the fifties was that we were acquiring an education to enable us to be better wives and mothers. We would be able to talk intelligently with our husbands on topics related to their business careers and we would be prepared to educate our children for a better life. A cliché from that era was: "Educate a man and you educate one person. Educate a woman and you educate an entire family." We believed that our liberal arts education prepared us to be well-rounded people. Few women went on for higher degrees. In 1955 the number of all women in the United States receiving bachelor's degrees was 101,000; master's degrees, 19,000; and doctoral degrees, 900.[3]

Getting married was equally, indeed probably more,

important than acquiring a degree for the young woman attending college. Each year the final issue of the Mundelein College *Skyscraper,* the newspaper of the small liberal arts college I attended, carried a series of group pictures. Traditionally one set of pictures was of all the honors graduates, while another was of all the graduates who were engaged to be married. The picture of the brides-to-be generally found its way into the Chicago daily papers, informing the public that educated women also marry. Among the student body it was considered much more of a distinction to be a prospective bride than an honors graduate.

Paradoxically, those of us attending college during those years were encouraged to acquire the wisdom, skills, and attitudes that would help us live, as one scholarship recipient was reminded, "honorably, intelligently, generously, graciously, influencing others for the good and bulwarking the religious, domestic, and civic life of the nation." Although emphasis was placed on acquiring an excellence in one's field, the equally heavy emphasis on the ultimate goal for most women, marriage, served as a counter-influence for the college woman. In 1954, when Mundelein conferred its Magnificat Medal on the outstanding Catholic college alumna, the students were more concerned that she was still unmarried than they were impressed by the fact that she was a doctor. Another year, when the college conferred the medal on a mother who was quite active in civic and charitable affairs, the students criticized her because her young sons were away in boarding school and she was involved in activities outside the home.

An article in the school paper telling how one alumna coped with a personal tragedy, describes her prior to an attack of polio. The description is an appro-

priate view of the attitude of the Catholic liberal arts
college woman in the 1950s:

> What more could a girl want? During her senior year at
> Mundelein . . . already SAC president, received the addi-
> tional honor of being elected May Queen. After graduation
> she taught school for a few years, then married . . . and
> honeymooned in Europe.
> They lived in Chicago for a few years and then moved to
> Denver, where he held a position with an insurance com-
> pany. . . .
> By 1952 their happy home included a pretty mother, a
> handsome father, eight healthy youngsters, a new car, a
> deep freeze, and an automatic washer.

And so it is little wonder that a woman graduating
from college in the mid-fifties, as I did, would plan to
work only until my first baby was born. Nor was it
unusual for me to declare that I would return to work
only if my family were in need. Some form of volunteer work would be the only acceptable outlet. And no
one ever suggested that perhaps some of us had career
talents that were valuable to society and should be used
even while raising a family. Family and motherhood
were too sacred to be shared with a career, even on a
short-term basis.

Thus when we married and moved to the suburbs
we were throughly conditioned and quite content to
dedicate our lives to being full-time wives and mothers.
When I questioned the women from the Ladies' Theology program concerning their life goals at the time
of marriage, all agreed that being happy in marriage
and having children were the only plans they had had
at that time. As one woman observed, "I just never
thought beyond that point." Another commented that
she never thought of things in terms of goals in those

days. She did "want to have a happy marriage, be a good wife, and I guess I hoped I'd have an interesting and fulfilling life." Beyond that her concern was to encourage her husband in building his dental practice.

We all readily accepted the divisions of functions which, we had been told, arise from different natures of man and woman. An example of this division, so ingrained in us, was found in the *Basic Cana Manual:*

(a) Woman is made for motherhood, physical or spiritual. Her whole psychological and emotional nature, as well as her physical, is adapted to having and rearing children; the fact of childbirth is not an isolated biological function, but involves woman's whole nature.

(b) Man is made for fatherhood, for life in the world, as breadwinner, as molder of the material universe.[4]

We also accepted the Cana doctrine that the desire for affection is woman's most dominant need, along with the fact that we are tender, sympathetic and sensitive. Because of this, we want to give ourselves to someone rather than to a cause. Our biggest dread is loneliness which is why we are so friendly to the people we encounter in the neighborhood and why we join bridge clubs and other social organizations. In fact, according to this view, the "desire to feel useful, needed, occupied, is as strong as any financial motivation in leading married women to work outside the home."

Our Protestant neighbors who moved to the suburbs at the same time shared our ideas on woman's role, if not on family size. Those belonging to churches with a strong conservative tradition were taught that the position of woman was God-ordained and that the successful Christian family depended upon the mother being in the home, guiding her family in God's way. As Ella May Miller, a broadcaster of "Heart to Heart" messages to radio audiences states:

God created woman primarily to be a "helper" and most women marry. But those who don't marry usually have the job of homemaker—for a parent, or brother, with another girl, or even for themselves. So really the basic principles or attitudes necessary for happy, successful homemaking apply to all women.[5]

A woman is a complement to a man; and it is her duty, in Mrs. Miller's opinion, to make a success of her marriage by recognizing and fulfilling his needs for acceptance, admiration and appreciation.

A woman was counseled to obey her husband even when it went against her better judgment, since she is *his* wife, living in *his* home, caring for *his* children. She was discouraged from seeking any self-actualization since this is a rebellion against the will of God. Books and articles encouraged wives to pretend husbands always know best, even when this is not true. A woman should never let on that she is more intelligent or gifted than her husband, but should allow him to think that her clever ideas are his own. This idea of submissiveness, which is based on Ephesians 5 with its admonition of "wives be subject to your husbands," gave a Christian blessing to the cultural view that the divisions of functions arise out of the different natures of man and woman. It also encouraged the young woman entering marriage to seek her fulfillment in life through the satisfaction she would provide for her husband and through passing on the life of faith to her children. The model of the self-sacrificing wife and mother was held up to the future suburban housewife as the ideal.

And the suburbs grew and were populated with women whose goal in life was to be a superior wife and mother. Even when they acquired innumerable conveniences to relieve them of the drudgery of housework, and sometimes even acquired household help to decrease their work load, they continued to strive to be perfect housewives. This was what they had been conditioned to be and this is what they felt they must be. Any doubts about this position were pushed aside as harmful to the marital relationship and damaging to the welfare of their children. A woman's free time was spent in learning how to be an even *better* wife and mother, with a heavy emphasis on *mother*. Dr. Spock became a second bible for most suburban mothers who were cut off from close family ties. No one could accuse the suburban woman of not being a conscientious mother. She also tried, as best she could, to work at making her marriage a success. The innumerable articles on how to have a successful marriage were eagerly read by the suburban housewife. If at times, because of the lack of time she was able to spend with her commuting and traveling husband, she experienced difficulties in carrying out the counselors' advice, she could not be faulted for not having tried.

Then sometime around 1963 a new attitude began to emerge. Betty Friedan wrote *The Feminine Mystique,* identifying the "problem that had no name," the boredom of the suburban housewife. Andrew Greeley published *Letters to Nancy,* encouraging Catholic women to develop their talents and establish an identity prior to marriage, so as to avoid seeking their entire fulfillment from the lives of their husbands. The Cana Conference commissioned a study and discovered that marriages did not suffer when the bride worked.[6] Moral theologians began questioning the Church's position on rhythm and some even wondered aloud what moral difference there was between rhythm and artificial forms of birth control. The ordination of women in some Protestant churches challenged the God-ordained inferior position of women.

The late 1960s found these changing attitudes toward the woman's role developing momentum. The Women's Liberation Movement in its various phases represented the most outspoken symbol of the fight for equality for women. Though many suburban women have been vehement in their opposition to most of the demands of the movement, there has been continual attention in the media, through educational programs, in politics, business and the church to the expanding dimensions of the woman's role.

In the 1970s we find the three principal women's magazines, *McCall's, Redbook,* and *Ladies' Home Journal* all featuring columns and articles dealing with the changing image of woman. The Second Vatican Council emphasized responsible parenthood, and, in spite of the encyclical letter *Humanae Vitae,* a large percentage of both clergy and laity in the American Catholic church accept the morality of some form of artificial birth prevention. The Cana Conference handbook for engaged couples has been revised to state that:

Husband and wife both have spheres in which by talent, competence and interest they exercise major authority. In common matters the husband will most often be the spokesman of authority but the wise husband will speak only after consultation, dialogue, and a consensus has been achieved. *Less than in former days, will the wife hide from her social responsibilities behind the excuse that she cannot speak until she has consulted her husband. . . .* She, within the freedom of which their life is made will know "their" mind on all subjects as well as will her husband.[7]

Protestant and Catholic churches are establishing special commissions to study the role of woman, and though there is considerable foot-dragging among many denominations, others are making serious efforts

to eliminate sexual discrimination. In 1964 when I
started my theological studies at the University of Chicago Divinity School, there were only three or four
women students. The 1975 winter quarter enrollment
included fifty-eight women out of a total of 244 students.

Though the number is small, women are now being
ordained and serving in pastoral roles in some Protestant churches. In a 1974 summary of the status of
women clergy, Scanzoni and Hardesty note:

On the level of officially ordained clergy, women are
scarce. Though some eighty Protestant denominations
around the world do ordain women, not more than 5 per-
cent of the ministers in these churches are women—though
in every denomination more than half of the members are.
And these denominations comprise a small minority of all
Christians. The largest groups, which rely heavily on tradition—Roman Catholicism, Orthodoxy and the Anglican
Communion—do not ordain women. Nor do many evangeli-
cal and fundamental groups.[8]

Women's colleges are offering courses in business
management and special degree programs for "older"
women who wish to continue their education once
their children are grown. My alma mater, Mundelein
College, is one of the forerunners in such programs
for adult women. The president of the college, Sister
Ana Ida Gannon, is a strong supporter of the ERA,
much to the consternation of many of her former students.

And it is little wonder why her action and the other
enumerated changes are of major concern to the suburban housewife. She is confronted with a situation for
which she is entirely unprepared. Her goal at the time
of her marriage was to spend the rest of her life as a

good wife and mother. Now she is either experiencing, or being made conscious of the possibilities of experiencing, new opportunities for expanding her role as a woman. She has long periods of time not needed for the care of her home and she is free to determine how she will use that time. But she is not prepared to make a decision about what to do. Many of the socially oppressive attitudes towards women are changing, providing opportunities for her to move into new roles in society either in the job market or volunteer work. But still she retains her idea that a woman's place is in the home. A new understanding of sexuality and religion offers her opportunities to make many decisions on her own in these areas. But her training has conditioned her to accept a submissive role in relation to men.

Consequently, the suburban woman is faced with a dilemma. She may hold fast to her ideals concerning "a woman's place is in the home," but she is subjected to enormous pressures to do something more with her time, as one woman told me. If she succumbs to these pressures she finds herself with few guidelines about what that "something more" might be. Today's suburban woman has no role models, which is one explanation for the various types of behavior described at the beginning of this chapter. What seem to be apparent contradictions are often only different individuals' attempts to deal with the turmoil they are experiencing as the mythical world of salvation for the suburban housewife is being challenged.

As we move on to a more thorough investigation of the present experience of the suburban woman, we must keep in mind that her conditioning has not prepared her for this situation. If we find her saying one thing while acting in a completely contradictory manner we must realize that the strength of a social myth lies in the fact that it supports desires, needs, and fears. It is capable of using facts as well as ignoring and distorting them in order to project its own air of plausibility and persuasion. The suburban woman subscribed to the myth of woman's place for a variety of reasons. If it constituted the source of meaning for behavior which is now questionable, she can be expected to react strongly to any challenge to its validity.

Nor is the turmoil concerning the changing role of woman confined to the suburban woman between the ages of thirty-five and fifty. As recently as fall of 1973, DePaul University undergraduate males continued to stereotype their female counterparts as inferior in intelligence, judgment, and ability to lead and assume responsibility. The majority of these young men said they did not want their wives to work once they started a family, nor did they wish to be involved with a female who earns more money than themselves. In the days of the energy crisis they suggested that when both a husband and wife require a car to get to work, the wife should quit her job.

Social myth dies hard. Indeed, as Elizabeth Janeway maintains, that which will prevail against inappropriate myths is "Not logic alone, and not compulsion, but instead an answer *in reality* to those needs which the myth answers in fantasy."[9] It is our task to determine if there is a Christian response which offers a realistic answer to the mythical world of the suburban woman.

3
Women Encounter Freedom

In the spring of 1973, I taught a mini-course to a group of Park Ridge women on the subject of a pastoral theology of suburban women. One of the participants objected strongly to the designation *suburban* women. She maintained that there was little, if any, difference between women in suburbia and their counterparts in the city. As an example she cited the fact that so many mothers in the suburbs were working. "All you have to do is spend a day trying to find someone to act as a schoolroom mother, and you'll realize that many Park Ridge mothers have left the home."

I agree that we have much in common with women in the urban setting; in fact we might have more similarities than differences. However, the situation we are examining here is that of women living in a suburban setting. If the conclusions we arrive at apply to the urban woman, then perhaps our pastoral theology will be useful to those engaged in an urban setting.

I do not agree, however, that the mere fact that the suburban woman is working indicates that there is no difference between us and our urban counterparts. We do not have the crowded living conditions and safety concerns of the urban poor and middle class. Neither do we have the ready access to the intellectual and cultural advantages of the city that the more affluent urban woman has. In addition we have, as one woman put it, "the pressure of being over-involved with our children when we are forced to be both mother and father." This is especially difficult for the suburban woman who is not originally from the surrounding metropolitan area or who has moved to a suburb a great distance from family support groups. This "loneliness of isolation" was cited by a number of women as a disadvantage of suburban living.

Yet one of the priests I interviewed saw the advantages of life for the suburban woman as including "the freedom . . . financial, intellectual and emotional security . . . to follow their personal interests." At the same time he saw this advantage as the possible cause of some of the disadvantages of her life, such as "keeping up with others and the resultant strains on a marriage. . ."

As we examine the situation of today's suburban woman we will observe that a good deal of her behavior is a response to the demands being made upon her as a result of this freedom. The range of this response goes all the way from the celebration of the submissive wife in the manner of *The Total Woman* to the abandonment of one's family to "find" oneself in a radical feminine commune. The majority of suburban women tend more towards the former than the latter. There are few thriving chapters of NOW (National Organization of Women) in most suburbs, but there are an increasing number of courses dealing with "Fascinating Womanhood" and the "Total Woman." When I spoke recently to the Ecumenical Women's Center in Chicago about the number of inquiries they received from suburban churches for their programs on feminism, they indicated there was little interest.

Who is this suburban woman, then, this person for whom we are attempting to develop a theological vision? How can we describe her, especially if she does not fit any particular mold? How can a minister who has been led to believe that the term *lady* is an archaic reminder of a bygone era possibly minister to a group of women who so identify themselves?

The problem of defining the suburban woman is similar to the problem encountered by Emily James Putnam in 1910 when she wrote the classical study, *The Lady*. According to Putnam, "The lady is proverbial for her skill in eluding definition," and for the purpose of her study she described the lady "as the female of the favoured social class." Putnam's further comments on the lady are appropriate as we try to place the situation of the suburban woman into a focus we are able to understand:

Every discussion of the status of woman is complicated by the existence of the lady. She overshadows the rest of her sex. . . . She is immediately recognised by everyone when any social spectrum is analyzed. . . . Economically she is supported by the toil of others; but while this is equally true of other classes of society, the oddity in her case consists in the acquiescence of those most concerned. The lady herself feels no uneasiness in her equivocal situation, and the toilers who support her do so with enthusiasm. She is not a producer; in most communities productive labour is by consent unladylike. On the other hand she is the heaviest of consumers, and theorists have not been wanting to maintain that the more she spends the better off society is. . . . Very dear to her is the observance that hedges her about. In some subtle way it is bound up with her self-respect and with her respect for the man who maintains it, that life would hardly be sweet

without it. When it is flatly put to her that she cannot become a human being and yet retain her privileges as a non-
combatant, she often decides for etiquette.[1]

Although those of us who are suburban women do
not necessarily consider ourselves the "favoured social
class," relative to many others, we come close to Putnam's description. Our technological servants toil for
us without complaint as long as they are properly maintained. In most instances our husbands have not only
acquiesced in their role of supporter, but they also consider this role an important part of their masculinity.
Though an increasing number of us are returning to
the work force, we do not tend to think of ourselves as
the producers of the society. We are, however, among
the heaviest consumers, as the rapid growth of suburban shopping centers indicates. The old story about a
woman buying something new to cheer up her de-
pressed spirits is the basis for the enormous pressure
advertising puts on the suburban woman to have the
newest and the best of everything.

There is a woman in our community who is said to
redecorate her house from scratch every three years.
The wife of a wealthy lawyer, with all her children in
school, she has found this to be one way to occupy her
free hours. Other women spend large amounts of time
shopping for the latest fashions in clothing for themselves and their children. Some even see that their husbands are dressed in the latest men's fashions. Eco-
nomic forecasters were concerned about the tendency
of the suburban woman to buy less in the period of the
1974–1975 recession. "After Christmas" sales and tre-
mendous savings at February sales in suburban stores
attest to the fact that our cutting back during the 1974
Christmas season hurt the retailer.

The suburban women whom I interviewed and who come to the School for New Learning are searching for an answer to what it means to be a woman in the contemporary world. Though their approach is different than that of radical feminists, it is unfair to regard them, as some feminists do, as women who refuse to see the situation. The pastoral minister who is new to the suburban situation, especially if he or she is fresh out of a stimulating university setting, might tend to dismiss suburban women as rather dull and, at times uninteresting. They are not always an exciting group of people who are actively and creatively contributing to the building of a better world. The minister must bear in mind that most people in our society are not highly-motivated, goal-oriented and committed. It is this problem of uncrystallized life which should be examined with an open mind before theology can begin to shed light on a Christian response to the situation.

The suburban women I deal with are part of the "uncrystallized" middle-class. Helena Lopata, in her important study of the contemporary woman, *Occupation: Housewife,* aptly describes them as housewives who:

> . . .with a bit more education and some skills for interacting with others is happier about her community, although still feeling powerless in her relation to the society. . . . She expresses a desire to organize life around her rather than just passively adjusting to it, but she still lacks sufficient knowledge to anticipate the consequences of various lines of action and then act in accordance with long range plans. She is changing her lifestyle, although often wishing for formulas to solve emerging problems.[2]

The problems of coping with a changing lifestyle are evidenced by the difficulty these women have in articulating personal goals for the immediate and distant fu-

ture. When I questioned the women about their three
most important personal goals for the next ten years,
only three of the ten interpreted this as referring to
them as individuals and not as part of the family unit.
Six hoped they would grow in their marital relationships and that their children would find happiness.
Five hoped to find some type of "personally satisfying
job." As one over-forty woman put it:

I'm really interested in finding some kind of work which
will be interesting and rewarding. Whenever I hear about
someone doing something different, that sounds enjoyable, I
try to find out more about it. I guess this is a luxury that we
have that our husbands certainly never did. I can just wait
until I find something that strikes my fancy. I don't have to
work, but I feel that I'd like to. I've been doing volunteer
activities for years now, and I just feel it would be more
rewarding for me to get into a job. I also want to be free to
travel, so it would have to be something which would allow
me some free time.

The luxury of choosing a job that will be interesting
seems to create a problem for some. As one 37-year-
old mother of three school-age children commented, "I
want to be fulfilled through something, but I'm not
sure what it is. Maybe I'll do volunteer work or take
some courses. I know I have to do something, but I
don't know what I can do well." Another replied, "I
want to create an intellectual challenge for myself."
One woman who listed as one of her goals, "to stay
away from work," also hoped to "gain more confidence
in knowing that what I'm doing is right. I'm hung up
on authority, and I really need to have some confidence that when I make a decision it's right."

Although none of the other women explicitly stated
this need for approval, it was implied as they struggled
to articulate how they would go about achieving their

goals. They recognized their inability to assure that their children will have happy lives. They know fairly well how their marriage relationship is progressing. They also recognize that both partners have to decide they want to grow if the relationship is to develop. They are frightened as they witness the breakup of marriages they had considered stable. There is no clear picture in their minds of what they should do to find the personal fulfillment they are seeking. They are a part of the cultural problem Lopata describes when she states:

... most Americans older than twenty-five have not been socialized into sufficient self-confidence and competence to enable full expansion of the self into creatively developed roles in the community and society. The lack of competence is a consequence of cultural change, of weakness in societally institutionalized training sequences, and of the person's own movement from one life style to another.... the demands and difficulties facing the woman are especially difficult because of the criticisms directed upon her.

These women are particularly affected by this problem of uncrystallization because they "have not been socialized to plan for a long life beyond the role of mother to young children." The suburban housewife who is no longer required to give as much time to her children and who has accepted "the stereotype of American women ... becomes worried over the gap between freedom from ---- and freedom to ----."[3]

This lack of ability to plan their lives around long-range goals elicits a variety of responses. Most suburban housewives become involved in a variety of activities. When I spend a morning phoning eight housewives and no one answers, I realize that "woman's place is in the home," is rapidly losing what little statistical validity it had. Even the non-working woman is not in her home.

Eight of the ten women I interviewed spend anywhere from eight to forty hours a week in activities outside the home. Four estimated that they fell into the eight- to fifteen-hour category while the other four guessed that it varied between twenty-five and forty hours. Some of the hours are spent in child-oriented functions, serving as scoutleaders, teacher aides, and playground mothers. But there is a wide range of other activities, including: tennis, exercise clubs, work with retarded children, lessons in art, sewing, and guitar, and involvement in the National Council of Christians and Jews. Much of that time is spent in church-related activities.

Given the many activities in which these women are involved and considering the role of the suburban mother as chauffeur for the children, one woman's comment that "I go to the beauty parlor once a week for a retreat," sums up the busy lives that many suburban women lead. It also suggests that some of the activities are not always as enjoyable as they appear. Perhaps with a greater sense of direction some of these women would find enjoyment in being the "master of one."

An increasing number of women are beginning to look for jobs. Most say that they must work if they want their children to get the best college education. And many of them are just "looking for a little something to pick up some extra money." Few are seeking jobs in areas which are related to their training and talents. Some feel that the present demands of family life would not allow them to work at a job that would require an additional commitment. Others, however, think they have no ability that would be useful in a work situation.

There is a self-confidence necessary to be successful

in roles in addition to that of a wife and mother which has not been cultivated by the majority of suburban women. As one 37-year-old mother of seven observed, "I think women should receive equal pay for equal work, but I would never want the responsibility _____ has in his job." In some instances this might indicate irresponsibility. It could also be an indication that this woman, who performs many volunteer functions in a competent and responsible manner in addition to managing an extremely well-organized household and doing part-time work, lacks the self-confidence to assume that she could manage the responsibilities of her husband's job. Whatever the reason, most of the women I talk with who are considering returning to work, do not seriously want to prepare themselves for another career.

The exception to this is the woman who has decided to return to college with a definite career choice in mind. At the School for New Learning we offer a three-day seminar to help adults planning to return to college define their educational goals and learn about our program. At the workshops offered in our suburban center, there is always a group of housewives who want to prepare for a life beyond that of mother of young children. All adults considering a return to a college environment require a good deal of confidence-raising. In addition, suburban women usually require more help in the area of goal-setting. Most come wanting a degree, but few have decided on a study program or what career they want. A pattern has begun to emerge where we are able to identify certain women who are simply going through the motions of looking for something to do. I have been on numerous panels for women at various colleges around Chicago, and increasingly I encounter women whom I would classify as professional "seekers." Someone has told them, or they have read somewhere, that going back to school is a way to find fulfillment. Just as one woman was looking for the perfect job, some women are looking for the perfect school. Neither exists.

Needless to say, since I am associated with an adult college, I am in favor of women gaining the academic skills which will enable them to live productive lives once the demands of young children no longer require their energy. Nevertheless, I am aware that many adult women are powerless to make decisions regarding changing lifestyles. Such women are looking for the new myth of salvation to replace the one they have been told is no longer effective.

Human-potential seminars, consciousness-raising groups, and Transactional Analysis are some of the new salvation cults which are attracting women who have developed a sense of discontent with their situation as housewives. Having witnessed some devastating experiences a few years ago among people who considered sensitivity training the answer to all relationship problems, I must admit to a certain degree of skepticism. I find many of the women who are most enthusiastic about these programs place a heavy emphasis on the need for self-fulfillment, to the exclusion of all other responsibilities.

Self-actualization and self-fulfillment are certainly important concepts in the development of a healthy personality. Unfortunately many women leave a consciousness-raising seminar convinced that their husbands are responsible for their own lack of achievement. The results of such attitudes are beginning to show in the increased number of women who decide that they are not free to "find" themselves within their marital relationship and conclude that divorce is the only solution for them. Though it is undoubtedly true that a large number of marital relationships are stifling experiences for both partners, divorce is not necessarily the guarantee that an unfulfilled woman will be free to find fulfillment. A sad testimony to the increased incidence of women leaving their families to find themselves is found in an article entitled "Husband Dumping." The author identifies the underlying causes of this action:

The message came through loud and clear: live fully in the moment, deal with your fears and hostilities, accept responsibility for your actions, realize your capacities, do your own thing, and above all, *tell the truth.* Unlike our parents' generation, which put duty before happiness ("Think of the children!"), we were urged to think of ourselves first, and let the chips and children fall where they may. Sanctioned by the human potential movement, which carried almost religious overtones, the new openness often fanned marital discord, since none of us could deal very "maturely" with revelations of infidelity—especially ongoing, protracted, wifely infidelity.

Beneath the bravado and the explosive effect of the human potential movement was an underlying, pervasive consciousness of the reality of death. In an era of broken illusions about the infinite possibilities of the American Dream, many middle-class adults, especially those in their thirties, seem to be reacting as medieval and Renaissance people did when confronted with the bubonic plague: eat, drink, and fornicate, for tomorrow we die.[4]

The discovery that many suburban women are making about their new opportunities for freedom is probably the single most important reason for the great discontent present in the suburban family. Any suburban minister who thinks the only marital problems within his church are those in which at least one member of the couple comes to him for advice is not listening to what is happening in the homes within his community. I know of few marriages where the couple are growing in their relationship. Indeed, as the couples enter their forties, I find more and more marriages to be destructive relationships, with toleration the only virtue being practiced.

Most married couples would quickly deny that this is true of their relationship. Nonetheless, if the pastoral theologian is responsible for recognizing what is going on before the group is even able to identify it to itself, the area of marital relationships is one which should receive immediate attention.

In June and July of 1973 our parish offered a series of talks on marriage for couples. The speaker was a priest who had been visiting the parish over a period of two or three summers while attending a graduate program at Loyola University. It was an extremely hot summer season and the talks were to be held in the gym, which was not air-conditioned. Nevertheless, over three hundred people attended the six weekly lectures. He offered little new in the way of insights into marital relationships, yet the people continued to come. It seems to me that this was a loud and clear message from the members of the parish that they were looking for advice and counsel from their church on the topic of marriage.

Women are generally the first to sense a need for growth within their marriage, especially as they have increased time to reflect on their situation and if they are involved in programs which address the topic of marriage. As one participant in the Ladies' Theology program remarked:

I really remember that session at Community Church when the priest spoke on communication and friendship in marriage. That really had an effect on our marriage. I remember coming home and saying to _____ "Here we've been married all these years and we're not really friends, because when we discussed the three people we would confide in if we had a serious problem, you weren't one of them. And that was because I know you'd be too critical." That sure got us talking and I think had a good effect on our marriage.

Fortunately, this woman's husband was willing to discuss the possibilities of improving their relationship. According to one of the parish priests, this is not always the case. He maintains that he spends a good deal of time "applying Band-Aids" to marriages where the woman has discovered opportunities for growth in her life, usually through participation in the Ladies' Theology Program, and her husband is not responsive.

During the period of my participation in the program, I knew this was one of the biggest problems faced by the women who were actively participating as discussion leaders. As one of them said:

I think it threatens a husband when he finds his wife going out and doing things and growing and thinking along other lines. . . . I think men are much happier if their wives are home. . . . I also think we began realizing that there was more to marriage since we got into Ladies' Theology . . . wanting friendship from our husbands. This threatens them.

Some husbands began to express a concern that they were not as knowledgeable as their wives on religious matters. A group of men, whose wives were among the early discussion leaders, joined together some five years after the start of the women's program to form an all-male program. They felt that their wives were so well-versed in theology at that point that the women would dominate a male-female group.

For a woman who does not wish to be considered the

type who would attempt to dominate a group that has male members, an alternative to programs such as the Ladies' Theology group or consciousness-raising seminars is offered in many Protestant churches. Protestant denominations have a long history of Bible study groups and women have participated in these for many years. The new dimension being offered in some of the conservative churches, and beginning to attract attention in what are considered more liberal communities, centers around the woman understanding her relationship to her husband based on the biblical directive that a wife should be submissive to her husband.

One such course, entitled "Fascinating Womanhood," is based on the book by Helen B. Andelin, a California mother of eight, which provides a plan for women wishing to be ideal wives. As the course proceeds, women are taught that they should have reverence for their husband as the leader, protector and provider. The wife should cultivate childlike and trusting qualities, be a competent housekeeper, not wear drab or unfeminine clothes and radiate happiness. As one of the teachers of this program says, "Women can't be leaders. God didn't set it up that way. The male ego doesn't allow the woman to be leader in the house."[5]

According to this program women must establish priorities, making the husband the top priority. Women should not be concerned about their rights in marriage but should understand that submission to their husband is not submission to tyranny. If the husband and wife are secure in their relationship, the man will not make unreasonable demands in his role as leader. The instructor maintains that, "If you really love a man and have a good relationship, submission isn't hard."

One participant in the Ladies' Theology program attended a similar course entitled "The Christian Woman" at a local conservative community church. She spoke admiringly of the woman who conducted the series. The lecturer had discovered through reading the Bible that the husband was the head of the family, and she had reoriented her lifestyle to allow this to be the case in her home. An example she gave to illustrate her complete relinquishment of leadership centered around a ride to the airport. They were late in leaving to pick up an out-of-town guest. The route her husband chose would take them at least a half-hour longer than the route she would have taken. Prior to her recognition of his leadership role, the lecturer would have told her husband how to go. However, with her new understanding she remained silent and they took the longer route, arriving even later than they had anticipated.

The woman reporting this to me said that though she admired the woman's action she had some difficulty relating to this account, since: "My husband has always been the decision maker and boss in this family, so it wasn't necessary for me to make such an adjustment." She found it difficult, however, to heed the advice of the speaker that women should look to their husbands for the spiritual leadership of the family. In the opinion of the participant, "Most men in this community don't seem to have the time to be concerned about spiritual matters. Although ____ cares about his faith, if I were to leave the spiritual leadership of the family up to him, I'm afraid we'd be in a bad way."

My final example of this cult of submissiveness provides an insight into what I consider to be the crux of the problem of the contemporary woman struggling with the changing character of the world and of her life. Marabel Morgan, a 38-year-old Florida housewife

and mother of two, shares her formula for a happy
marriage in *The Total Woman*,[6] a bestseller in both
hard-back and paper editions. Marabel married Char-
lie expecting to have a perfect marriage, but after
about six years of married life she began to sense that
things were not going well. At this point she embarked
on a thorough search of all the literature she could
uncover on the topic of marriage, including the Bible,
and discovered that the cause of their unhappiness
rested in the fact that she had failed to understand her
role.

After she had experienced amazing results in her
own marriage with a change in her attitude, she began
to share her formula with friends. Eventually she developed a course which she and over 100 of her graduates
teach all over the country. The book, which has over
200,000 copies in print, contains Morgan's formula,
along with examples of how students have put it to use
and improved their own marriages. It also contains a
series of assignments at the end of each part which
should help the reader be a more organized woman,
accepting and admiring wife, ideal sex partner, understanding mother, and woman of faith.

The key to improving the marital relationship rests
in a woman learning to accept her husband, admire
him, adapt to him and appreciate him. Using Sarah,
Abraham's wife, as a model Morgan counsels:

It is only when a woman surrenders her life to her husband, reveres and worships him, and is willing to serve him,
that she becomes really beautiful to him. She becomes a
priceless jewel, the glory of femininity, his queen![7]

Because the Total Woman is a member of our modern society, Morgan also counsels her, in a section en-

titled "Sex 201," to begin to understand the importance of sex to a man. Since sex comforts a man,
women are encouraged to learn how to be happily married mistresses.

I must admit to experiencing a great deal of frustration while reading *The Total Woman,* something akin to
the frustration I felt when I read *Beyond God the Father.*
Both books had some valid points, yet both were too
simplistic in their conclusions. Sex is an important component of a happy marriage, and far too many suburban women are still suffering from the Victorian pru-
dishness of our mothers and grandmothers. It is also
important to keep the lines of communication open
between husband and wife, but the entire emphasis in
The Total Woman is on the woman burying her own
personality in order to allow her husband to be successful in his career. Testimonials from Total Men who
had been so pleased with their new wives that they had
taken them on vacations and bought them gifts are
used to show the elation husbands feel when their
wives adopt this attitude.

But at the end of the book I was left with the question, "What else is there for the woman?" If she follows
Morgan's directives and organizes her time well, there
is bound to be a considerable amount of time in her
day, especially when the children are gone, that must
be spent on something more than preparing to be a
mistress.

I was also struck by the fact that Marabel Morgan is
an extremely powerful woman, who either consciously
or unconsciously, is advocating that women deny their
power. Rollo May has written of the destruction that a
pseudo-innocence about power can cause for an individual and a nation.[8] I am increasingly convinced that
the opportunities for freedom that suburban women

are experiencing give them a great deal of power; power which frightens them because they have not been conditioned to use it in a constructive manner. Just as May claims that our country's denial of its power has dire consequences, I maintain that the suburban woman's denial of her opportunities to develop herself as a person constitutes a dangerous threat to her, her family and her community, and her country.

This same fear of power is, I believe, a partial motive for much of the anti-male behavior of the radical feminist. The radical feminist will admit that she has power, but she has been subjected to the same cultural conditioning as the Total Woman. Both of them are afraid of their power. The Total Woman denies she has it. The radical feminist fears that if she relates to a male from a position of power he will attempt to rob her of it. So she says, "Let us women go off by ourselves and work this out." She lacks the confidence that her power is the real thing and cannot be taken from her unless she willingly gives it up.

Neither of these attitudes is so surprising when we reflect on the image of a powerful woman that is present in the minds of most women and also most men. I can recall my own violent rejection of the label "a strong woman" when the priest who was working with us in the Ladies' Theology program told me that some of the other discussion leaders were having problems with me because I was such a strong person and had everything in my life under control. Part of my rejection of his comments sprung from the fact that many parts of my life were not all that organized; but, in retrospect, I realize that the idea of being thought a strong woman embarrassed me. One of the discussion leaders said she found it difficult to relate to me since I could accomplish so much and she felt inferior by comparison. She said I reminded her of an aunt who had the same qualities and had seriously damaged her cousins' lives and caused difficulties in this woman's life.

At that stage of my life I was entirely unequipped to deal with such observations. Fortunately, there were enough people who apparently did not have trouble relating to me, even if I were this strong woman, that I eventually could accept the fact that I had strength and a degree of power which I had not previously considered.

Although I can now admit that I do have a great deal of power and that I can use it for constructive purposes, my cultural conditioning still makes it difficult for me always to act from a position of power. When confronted with the need to meet demands in my work situation that are not always pleasant, such as deciding to reject an unqualified student for our program, I often wish I could assume a pseudo-innocence. When the work load is heavy, I wish I had never left the security of my home. When I fail to assert my professional position in a largely male-dominated situation, due to a lack of self-confidence, I wish I could withdraw with the few women whom I know understand how I feel. None of these attitudes is admirable, but it is crucial for those who are ministering to suburban women to realize that they do exist, as women are confronted more and more with increased opportunities for freedom. And Marabel Morgan and her group, with their ostrich-like approach, are not going to make these opportunities disappear. Smaller families, increased technological conveniences and longer life potentials are part of the life of the suburban woman. She might have difficulty coping with this situation; but, until she is aware of exactly what it is she is confronting and why she is having problems confronting it, the suburban woman will continue to exerpience a sense of frustration which could destroy her and her whole family structure.

The suburban woman is being faced with new opportunities for freedom; we have observed some of the consequences of these opportunities. We now turn to the Christian tradition. Is there anything there which might help the suburban woman understand her situation and begin to accept the responsibility which must accompany freedom, if this freedom is to have constructive, rather than destructive consequences?

4
Women in the Local Church

I am weary of the endless discussion on woman's place in the Church. Although I am neither anti-Bible nor anti-history, I am tired of being continually exhorted by feminists to look at the discrimination against women in the Bible and in the history of Christianity. I find it equally tiresome to be constantly reminded by anti-feminists, that the good wife in Proverbs had as her main concern the care of her husband, children and household. The examples of Sarah, Rebecca, Leah and Rachel are coupled with the admonitions of Paul concerning woman's subordination to support outcries against the dangers of women seeking a position of equality. Then, of course, there are the moderates who attempt to justify equality for women who use the examples of Deborah, Jael, Judith and Esther from the Old Testament, and Martha and Mary, Anna, The Woman at the Well and others from the Gospels, and Phoebe, Priscilla and Phillip's four daughters from the period of the early Church to show that despite the general cultural view of women in biblical times the situation is different in Judaism and Christianity.[1]

Such comparisons are of little value in solving the problems of how a woman should live in the second half of the twentieth century. A second reason I find many of these discussions not only tiresome, but also destructive, is that they eventually lead to the question of ordination of women. This is such an emotion-laden issue that it amazes me to hear many priests, who I consider liberal on other issues, firmly defend the position that, since Jesus chose only males for his apostles, it is theologically impossible to approve the ordination of women. The inability to separate the issue of responsible behavior for a Christian woman from the issue of ordination always seems to leave the former question unsolved.

I am not advocating that we ignore the Bible or the Christian tradition when we seek illumination on how contemporary suburban women can respond to new opportunities for freedom. What I am advocating, however, is that we expand our area of investigation from the traditional role of women in the Bible, to the search for an appropriate symbol within the history of Christianity which would put the situation of the suburban woman into a Christian framework. To accomplish this, it will be necessary to look to the Bible and to tradition. But we must first question how one lives a responsible Christian life, rather than what the role of woman is.

Although we have to admit that the biblical period was one of patriarchal dominance and that Paul was obviously reflecting the culture of his time, we cannot deny that Jesus addressed his message to all. Women, as well as men, were challenged at various points to accept him and his message. Even Paul, in his Letter to the Galatians (3:26–28), admits that all who are baptized in Christ have put on Christ. No longer are the ordinary distinctions of society relevant. Although distinctions in class, color, nationality and sex are not abolished when men and women become Christian, these distinctions are seen in a new light. All Christians, in their multitudinous varieties, are caught up in a new fellowship in Christ.

The question then becomes: Where does one live out this new fellowship one is caught up in with Christ? One lives out his or her Christian life in a community. That is what occurred once Jesus was no longer physically present to proclaim His message. His followers banded together to support each other in their new-found faith, to celebrate the Good News, and to proclaim it to others.

The contemporary suburban woman who identifies herself as a Christian also lives out her life within a community called a local church. For a Catholic suburban woman, this church is generally dictated by geographical boundaries established at the diocesan level. Protestant women have more freedom in choosing which church they will attend but, in most instances, both Protestant and Catholic women attend churches that are of the *family-structure* typology described by Colin Williams:

> In this structure all the members function as one family. Its main task is nurture of its members of all ages so that they may participate in God's mission in the world. Usually residential in character, the family-type structure serves a particular segment of God's world in which it is located.[2]

Williams does not feel that most present-day local churches are true to this type though they claim to minister to families. His complaint is that they are too large to be successful.

The Christian suburban woman is, in most instances, a member of a local or parish church. She may be a very active member, a moderately active member, or go once a year. Yet when she is asked her religious denomination and church affiliation, she generally names a church in the area where she lives.

The purpose of developing a pastoral theology of and for suburban women is not to try to find a formula that will work with all the women of a congregation. Rather, the purpose is to begin exploring what symbols might speak to those women who are interested in what the Christian message has to say about their lifestyle.

Before turning to the symbol of the local church in the Bible and Christian tradition, it would be helpful to examine the role the Church plays in the lives of many suburban women. For this purpose, I will rely heavily on the responses from the women who were involved in the Ladies' Theology program. These are the women who would probably be most ready to contribute to the development of a pastoral theology as well as appreciate what illumination the Christian tradition could offer her regarding her present situation.

Helena Lopata's in-depth interviews of housewives identified two sets of relationships in which many women were deeply involved:

Neighboring has been and is becoming a significant activity for many respondents, helping to solve the problems of loneliness and providing opportunities for the exchange of homemaking knowledge and the alleviation of anxieties felt in the role of mother, bringing the pleasure of adult companionship and leisure-time interaction. Also important to many women is friendship with selected individuals or couples begun in a variety of ways and gradually developed into more intimate and "fun-sharing" relations.[3]

The participants in the Ladies' Theology Program indicated that Mary, Seat of Wisdom parish has provided them with the opportunity to engage in neighboring with other women in the community and to develop couple-friendships. In addition to sharing their ideas with other women on topics of mutual concern in the Ladies' Theology program, the parish offers various other activities with opportunities for adult companionship and leisure-time interaction.

Each of the ten women was asked to consider the five couples they see most often and to tell where they first met each couple and where the couple now lives. Thirty-six of the fifty couples were found to live in Park Ridge and thirty of them are members of the parish. In a few instances, the couples had been acquaintances prior to moving to the parish and the friendship developed as a result of the proximity of their new homes.

This high degree of involvement with other parishioners might be attributed to the wide variety of social events offered by the parish. It might also indicate that, for some of the couples, the wife's involvement in a parish activity has led to social contacts with couples which, over the years, developed into couple-friendships. Whatever the reason, the response indicates that for these women there is a large degree of social involvement with others who live in the same parish. The parish is an important part of their lives.

When asked what they liked best about the parish, the women's overwhelming response was the feeling of community among the people and the open and friendly attitude of the priests. It is, as one woman commented, a "caring community. I always feel that the priests and other parishioners really care about what happens to me. It's a good feeling."

Women are actively involved in the parish. They estimate that 20–75% of parish women are involved in at least some parish activity. The clergy, however, estimated that between 15% and 40% of the women are active but their guess as to how many of the people active in the parish are women ranged from 55% to 75%, the pastor indicating the latter.

One woman's comment that the women "do just about everything" in the parish was echoed in the responses of the other women and clergy. Among the many functions mentioned were such things as: teachers' aides, fund-raisers, sacristans, scout leaders, cheerleaders and girls' sports coaches, lay ministers of communion, commentators and lectors at Mass, religious educators for the children attending public schools, and pre-school religion teachers. Women also do catering for special parish events, work with older parishioners, coordinate the social functions of the parish and perform acts of mercy in times of crisis. They are members of the parish council, the parish school board and the Home-School Association. They direct and produce the school plays as well as the adult variety shows, and lead many discussion groups. One woman observed cynically, "Women do all the hard-core work that men don't want to do."

In the opinion of both the clergy and the women, these activities play an important part in the lives of the women who engage in them. As one priest commented, "Their role in the parish has a big priority in their lives. It seems to come right after their obligations to their families and to their own private lives." He felt that a number of women might be more involved than they should be. Another priest indicated that some women need the parish for any life outside of the home.

The importance of the parish to the women is indicated by their response to what type of parish they would choose if they were forced to move. Catholics do not have the same degree of freedom in choosing a parish as many Protestants do. Some of these women said they had thought of moving but rejected the idea because of the parish. Three had moved, but stayed within the parish boundaries. One had moved from another Park Ridge parish to Mary, Seat of Wisdom, specifically because of its reputation.

While it is certainly true that Mary, Seat of Wisdom parish affords more opportunities for its women parishioners than many other local churches, this does not mean that other churches are unable to do the same. The spirit of Mary, Seat of Wisdom is a combination of the spirit of the laity and the spirit of the clergy. It has taken work on everyone's part; work that, if imitated elsewhere, could bring similar results. Cooperation does not always come easily in a large church community, but when everyone makes an effort good things are bound to result.

Paul Tillich maintains that there is a paradoxical relationship between the sociological and theological character of any church. It is utterly inadequate to judge a church (or a parish, since Tillich is referring to a particular church in space or time) only from the view of its sociological function and social influence. "A church which is nothing more than a benevolent, socially useful group can be replaced by other groups not claiming to be churches; such a church has no justification for its existence."[4] All parishes need to develop a theological vision which will unite the members in the common task of living the Christian life.

For Catholics who lived in metropolitan parishes in predominately Catholic areas prior to the mid-fifties, it made little difference in which parish you lived. The faith structure of all parishes was similar, and is described by John Shea as "the salvation of the individual soul through obedience to the laws of God and the Church and participation in the sacramental system."[5] This shared faith structure had a great cohesive force. It gave the members of the immigrant parishes and those to which their children and grandchildren belonged in the thirties, forties, and fifties, a sense of "belonging." This spirit went a long way towards helping the members establish their identity, not only within the parish, but also in the outside world of work or school.

It is this sense of belonging which is so important to the women of Mary, Seat of Wisdom. It is this sense of belonging which will be the starting point of our model of a local church which will be responsive to the needs of a suburban community. This model will also, hopefully, be faithful to the spirit of the local church as found in the New Testament and during the history of Christianity when the local church met the needs of the people. This vision will attempt to follow the direction of Shea's theological vision for a local church. It will try to be one which:

. . . emerges from the interaction of contemporary experience and religious tradition, shaping itself around the problems of the culture. It functions as servant and facilitator of Christian living. Theological vision also orientates man toward the future and gives direction to the innumerable and undifferentiated experiences of his life.[6]

My proposal for a theological vision of a local church which will address itself to the problems and experiences of middle-clas suburbia will be divided into three parts. The first of these parts considers the local church as *A Spirit-filled community*.

Today, there is increased awareness of the social character of man. This awareness can be found in all segments of culture, including the churches. An individual, alone, does not possess human nature since man is "essentially a community and he exists only insofar as genuine community is not a dream, but a reality."[7] Who among us does not long to be part of what Rollo May describes as authentic community?

Community is where I can accept my own loneliness, distinguishing between that part of it which can be overcome and that part of it which is inescapable. Community is the group in which I can depend upon my fellows to support me; it is partially the source of my physical courage in that, knowing I can depend on others, I guarantee that they also can depend on me. It is where my moral courage, consisting of standing against members of my own community, is supported even by those I stand against.[8]

It was this search for community which made the original course in the Ladies' Theology program one which many women recall fondly. During that time the membership in the program was limited to women from Mary, Seat of Wisdom parish, with a priest from the parish serving as group leader. A concerted effort was made to create an experience of community among the participants. The group eventually grew too big and the leaders, due to a lack of understanding of what constitutes community, were unable to keep the spirit alive. But for a fleeting period the members had a small taste of communion. As one woman commented some years later:

I really liked it best when we were a smaller group. It was like a faith experience . . . sharing, discussing, talking about the past, the present, and the future. We had an opportunity to grow in friendship. . . . It was nice having a priest from the parish involved. . . . It made it seem more of a community. . . . Once it got so big there was no feeling of unity. . . . When it was just women from the parish we often would run into each other between sessions, shopping or at a party, or at something at church and that helped reinforce what we had discussed at the sessions. . . . I really think that's one reason I dropped out . . . it just wasn't as personal anymore.

It is also the search for such authentic community which is the clarion call for all group movements which predominate in the contemporary world. What is singularly lacking in most attempts to build community, however, is the recognition of the ambiguity of all human communities. In order to have authentic community we need to be free people; and the very freedom which allows us to form community also forces us to accept the eventual breakdown of all communities.

Rollo May argues convincingly in *Power and Innocence* that the pseudo-innocence in our culture which causes us to hide from ourselves our capacity for evil eventually manifests itself in outbursts of violence. Our attempt to portray the "good guy" image leads to what May considers to be the inherent evil of our day: "Situations in which the person is prevented from taking such responsibility [for the effects of his own actions]."

How can the Church speak to a situation in which men and women who have the freedom to form community and earnestly search for community, are also afraid to acknowledge their contribution to the breakdown of community? This is of particular significance to a Church which has always recognized one of its main functions to be that of gathering people together to celebrate the Eucharist in a community.

Tillich, in his discussion of the ambiguities of the churches, said: "The Church shows its presence as Church only if the Spirit breaks into finite forms and drives them beyond themselves."[9] In other words, a church will only show itself as a church when it recognizes that, although it is a group of people gathering together to acknowledge their relationship to God, it can only do this by the power of the Spirit which Jesus has sent to keep His body alive. The Church is a community because God wills it to be one, because He chose to send His Son with the Good News, and because He continues to sustain men with His love.

The idea of a community which has been set free by the Spirit is true to the New Testament concept of the *ekklesia,* a Greek word meaning an "assembly of people" and implying the process of assembling as well as the assembly. The importance of its use by the early Christians flows from the fact that it is the Septuagint translation of the Hebrew word *kahal* which signifies the community gathered together by God, the Covenant community, the community of God. This *ekklesia,* the Remnant of Israel, is gathered into a special synagogue formed by Jesus' disciples. The New Covenant does not reject all the characteristics of the old, but claims for itself a new Spirit sent by Jesus after His death, resurrection and ascension. This Spirit will sustain the community as the bearer of the fullness of divine revelation.

The chief characteristic of the new community in the New Testament is that it centers around the Lord, in whose life it hopes to share. He directs its destiny and, although ascended, He will be in its midst when it gathers in His name (Matt. 18:20). It is this characteristic which suggests the second element of our theological vision for a local church.

The image of the parish community as a group of people who, in the freedom of the Spirit, are able to let authentic community develop, provides a model for overcoming the ambiguities which surround human community and which hinder the exercise of both freedom and responsibility. But this is not adequate. It does not identify that which allows the members to believe that they are a Spirit-filled community. We must expand our image to that of *a Spirit-filled community which knows through Jesus Christ of God's plan of salvation.*

As long as individuals and parish communities are unaware of the influences which are operative in their lives, they are neither free nor responsible. As long as a local church is in doubt about the significance of the Good News for its existence, it will remain a stagnant religious community and just another socially benevolent group.

The response of women to the Ladies' Theology program and to innumerable study programs offered in Protestant churches in our community demonstrates that the laity are interested in religious study when instruction is provided. As one woman noted, "I didn't know where I was religiously, and this was the most convenient way to learn." She had been educated in Catholic schools for sixteen years; and suddenly, with the advent of the Second Vatican Council, things seemed completely changed. With four small children, it was impossible for her to travel to a college course. She and another woman who "wanted to move religiously, but didn't know how," saw the offering of a nearby course on the Bible as an opportunity to begin exploring when and how to move.

Although the initial intent of the program had been to offer a strictly formal approach to learning, we included a period for discussion which all but one of the women I interviewed considered extremely worthwhile. This learning strategy provided the women with the opportunity to discover, as one woman put it, "that I wasn't the only one who was confused about what was going on in the Church."

The image of the local church as a community which is aware of God's love for man is in keeping with the image of the local church presented in Scripture. The entire mission of the New Testament community was to proclaim the message of salvation which Christ brought. Teaching was an important function in the New Testament Church. Once the *kerygma* was proclaimed, the teachers, chosen by the Lord and led by the Spirit (l Cor. 12:28ff; Eph. 4:11) guarded the tradition and engaged in pastoral-ethical instruction (Rom. 12:17). The object of Christian teaching is Christ (Eph. 4:21) and the teachers based their words on the original testimony of the apostles.

The tendency to gnosticism which could follow if we were to end our definition of the local church as the Spirit-filled community which knows through Jesus of God's plan of salvation, impels us to elaborate on the implications of that knowledge. According to Gregory Baum, an individual's knowledge of the mystery which controls his life leads to personal transformation.[10] So, too, a Spirit-filled community knowing of God's graciousness would have to respond to this knowledge. And the normal response to any good news in one's life is to want to share our awareness of the news and celebrate it with those close to us. For this reason we should expand our vision of a local church to a Spirit-filled community which knows, through Jesus, of God's plan of salvation and *proclaims this knowledge in celebration and fellowship.*

As the experience of the Ladies' Theology program indicated, in addition to attending the sessions and talking to others there about what they were learning, the participants also wanted to celebrate. A tradition was established at the initial series which lasted for four or five years. In the spring the women who participated in the program organized a concluding Mass and a catered dinner to which they invited their husbands and the parish priests and sisters. This desire to celebrate in fellowship with other participants and those close to us resulted from the understanding the women had gained concerning the role of liturgy and fellowship in the biblical church, as well as from a sense of exhilaration with the program.

The New Testament community proclaimed its knowledge of the redemptive mystery. This unity between Gospel and liturgy demands of a parish community that its liturgies be a celebration of the deepest dimensions of human life, and not mere routines to be suffered through each Sunday. Good liturgies should lead to an increased awareness of the meaning of the mystery and should encourage those who participate in them to be open to the presence of Christ and the Spirit in the midst of each celebration. The liturgy should, in addition to being a community's proclamation of the Good News, also serve as a catalyst for the transformation of life which results from the indwelling of the Spirit.

Karl Rahner maintains that only those activities which flow from the liturgy are the direct responsibility of the parish.[11] This Catholic position, in some instances, would not be acceptable for many of the decentralized Protestant churches. However, even in a Catholic parish the life of fellowship can be said to flow from the liturgy if this spirit of fellowship is the result of the decision of the members of the parish to trust in the Good News and allow the Spirit to enrich its community. Fellowship is a key dimension in keeping the life of faith alive in any denominational community.

The need for authentic community is present in every local church. It is somewhat acknowledged by those churches which become activity oriented. But the ambiguities of human life which cause us to draw back from authentic community hinder us in our search for ways to improve life in the local church. The fellowship demanded by Jesus—that we love one another as he has loved us—is the most demanding of encounters. Indeed, it is just as impossible for us to achieve as it is for the rich man to enter heaven. Nevertheless, all things are possible with God; so perhaps a local church which sees itself as a *Spirit-filled community aware of God's plan and proclaiming this in celebration,* might begin to explore ways in which we could become more aware of God's presence in its fellowship. One way to begin would be to identify the most obvious obstacles to fellowship and work at removing them, always aware of the ambiguity which confronts such an endeavor.

It takes more than sociological and psychological insight to make the Spirit more evident in a community, but such insight can be used to remove obstacles to realizing God's presence. Church projects of any type —be it parish council, fashion show, study group, prayer meeting or bowling—will not of themselves result in better human relations among the members of the community, but they can help. However, given our tendency to pseudo-innocence, these endeavors sometimes can lead to destruction of the parish or a loss of original enthusiasm.

Each fall the adults in our parish present a variety show, in which all the amateurs and some of the professionals within the parish perform for the enjoyment of the rest of us. For the past three years, the teenagers have done the same thing in the spring. These activities provide a great opportunity for parishioners to get to know each other. It is a chance for building real friendships, but unfortunately, it has also caused enmity and jealousy on the part of many.

This is one of the reasons why we must be cautious in evaluating the effectiveness of these activities as builders of Christian community. If these activities are not placed in a proper perspective, it becomes extremely difficult for the participants to separate what is church and what is strictly social. It then becomes even more difficult to acknowledge the anger and frustrations which, legitimately or illegitimately, arise while engaged in these endeavors. If it is difficult to acknowledge our tendency to evil in ordinary circumstances, how much harder it becomes when we are doing something "for the Church."

Parish activities are a legitimate way to develop the fellowship for which contemporary man is searching, as long as there is an awareness of the specific aim of the different activities. Awareness of the sociological character of the parish community is also crucial. When these are joined with a theological vision of the local church, a sense of identity emerges which is helpful in confronting the ambiguities of contemporary life.

A vision of the parish as *a Spirit-filled community which knows of God's plan of salvation through Jesus Christ and proclaims this knowledge in celebration and fellowship*, might appear quite different than the faith structure of some of the immigrant churches of the first half of this century. If such a vision meets the need of people desirous of communion, it could help create the same sense of belonging once found in the immigrant churches. It could be meaningful for a local church seeking to be more than a benevolent, socially useful group.

The Christian tradition of the local church as we know it today was not explicitly present in the New Testament communities; it did not develop until sometime at the end of the third or beginning of the fourth century. However, the notion of parish first appeared in the New Testament. The two types of communities found there, the charismatic and relatively unstructured Pauline community, and the more monarchical and sedentary church depicted in the Apocalypse were somehow merged to form a local, parish church presided over by a bishop of the city. By the beginning of the second century and until the fourth century, the priest's role was to proclaim the faith and teach the Word. The history of the parish from the fourth century until the Reformation and the Council of Trent was not a period of great emphasis on pastoral care. This was in some part attributable to the corruption of the official hierarchy, but also to the illiteracy of the ordinary Christian. Nonetheless, thousands of parishes existed in Western Europe where acts of mercy, worship and instruction offered the common people a sense of unity in their daily lives.[12] Corruption and abuses at the higher ecclesiastical levels, which eventually seeped down to the local levels, was a factor in the turning of great numbers to Protestantism. However, the unifying force of the local church was not ignored in the Reformation churches or in the reforms proposed at the Council of Trent.

The Council placed the responsibility for much-needed church reform on the parish and the diocese.

In theory, this should have contributed to the development of a theological vision of a parish. However, due to the spirit of the times, what actually resulted was the formation of individualistic parishes devoid of a deep sense of liturgical worship. Protestants, from Anglicans to Mennonites, have traditionally placed much greater emphasis on the initiative of the local church.

The system of local churches has survived into our present day as a means of keeping the faith of the Christian Church alive. The challenge which faces the leadership of the churches today is a challenge to continue to provide the opportunity, in an era of increasing despair, for this faith to live. To accomplish this, it is necessary to develop a vision of Christianity and of the Christian life which merges with the experiences of our present culture. This challenge will necessitate a variety of approaches in expressing differing visions for a local church, given the diversity of situations to be addressed.

The vision of a parish as *a Spirit-filled community which knows of God's plan of salvation through Jesus Christ and proclaims this knowledge in celebration and fellowship* is one which should facilitate the practice of Christian living for the middle-class suburbanite. It will also, I hope, give a direction to the next stage of our process—the development of strategies of action for the women who are members of these communites. By broadening the discussion of women's role in the church to include her full membership in a local church, our orientation will be one of building toward the future rather than one of repeating outmoded clichés or condemning the past.

5

Women Respond to Freedom

When my sixteen-year-old daughter read a description of Fascinating Womanhood's lesson in foot-stomping called, "How to be cute, even adorable, when you are angry,"[1] she observed, "I certainly don't need to take lessons in how to be angry, I've been slamming doors for years. Maybe I don't always look so cute, but it sure gives me lots of satisfaction." Julie's comments highlight the utter absurdity of a group of middle-aged women resorting to childlike tactics to make their husbands "love it." This makes me wonder what kind of opinions such women have of themselves and of their husbands which would cause them to seriously follow the advice of the gurus of Women's Submissiveness.

Even more frightening, as I reflect on Julie's reaction to this entire movement, is the image of women that we create for girls who look to us for role models. Today's woman, with her vacillation between the extremes of submissiveness and liberation, unable in either case to make commitments to responsible behavior, is not offering her daughters attractive options for a full life. Nor is she helping her sons formulate realistic expectations concerning future relationships with women. Most suburban women would agree that one of their most important tasks is to be a good mother, just as one of their chief goals is to ensure their children's future happiness. They fail, however, to see the connection between this ambiguous behavior and the future happiness of their children. This situation lends credit to Rollo May's theory that a person's inability to take responsibility for his own action is the inherent evil of our day.

Moreover, as we observed in our investigation of the lives of suburban women, they seem locked into a situation with little or no idea of how to find the magic key to peace and order. The search for creative response to opportunities for freedom goes on in a piecemeal, haphazard way. Since their particular situation is a new cultural phenomenon they, too, have no role models. When our mothers engaged in club activities to fill their spare hours it was because there was nothing else to do. While today's woman is aware, to some degree, that other options are available, she is paralyzed at the thought of setting concrete goals which require commitment. One freedom most suburban women definitely lack is the freedom which comes with self-confidence.

The Christian woman, who shares the vision of the local church as described in the previous chapter must, as a full member of the community, begin to evaluate her lifestyle in light of that vision rather than continue to rely on the various cultural and religious views that contributed to the creation of the prison of her mythical world. Such behavior demands that the Christian woman also be a *responsible woman*, always realizing that, for the Christian, Christ is the paradigm of responsibility.[2] Christ is the key which will unlock the prison.

Once a woman sees herself as living out the life of Christ in a Spirit-filled community, she will be free to risk the assumption of responsibility for her actions, aware that at times these actions are the cause of evil, but also aware of the forgiveness and love of God. This freedom which belief gives to a person is the most precious freedom a woman possesses, but it must not be locked up with her in the prison of her mind. It must be used to better understand her own situation and help others come to appreciate the same freedom. It is a freedom which requires response or it will be quickly lost or wasted away.

How does a woman act in a responsible manner? One of the most frequent questions we heard at the Ladies' Theology program from women who were developing an awareness of expanding opportunities was, "What do I do now?" There is *no one* Christian response to this question, but there are some guidelines which should prove helpful for a woman who is seriously considering new directions in light of a new Christian self-understanding. We must always be wary of the pitfall of laying out specific guidelines which *every* woman must follow in order to find the best way to live the life of Christ.

The crucial first step that all women must take, however, is the one of dropping the mask of pseudo-innocence. Opportunities for freedom pervade almost every aspect of our lives. Technology has given us the time and mobility to determine how we will allocate our time—at home, on the tennis courts, at a religious study program, in an art class or even on a job. Financial security has given us the luxury of "waiting for the right job to come along," or not working at all. The lessening of discrimination has made it possible for us to move into areas of business, religion and government previously considered off-limits. We are free to seek self-fulfillment. However, we must decide how we will respond to each of these freedoms. We cannot simply drift along letting fate, or our husbands, make the choices for us.

The simple child-like attitude cultivated by the Total Woman is an option that some might choose, but, if it is chosen, the woman must consider the full consequences of the choice. The *responsible woman* must bear in mind that she is a member of a much larger community than that of her immediate family. As a Christian she bears the responsibility of witnessing to others God's love. The world is no longer "man's world" with the males the only ones bearing responsibility for their actions. Since it is "man's and woman's world," we, too, must evaluate our lifestyle decisions from a more universal point of view.

Many women, as we mentioned earlier, have become heavily involved in consciousness-raising groups. A large number of the women I interviewed and those who come into our program are seeking self-fulfillment. But as the author of "Husband Dumping" observed, self-fulfillment must have limitations or it turns into self-destruction.

The problem of the self and of the individuality and loneliness that come with the recognition that we are selves separated from others is a rather recent problem in the history of the human race. Our primitive ancestors were incapable of imagining their existence apart from the particular group to which they belonged. Their social existence was also closely associated with nature; thus, self-conscious separateness was not an option.[3]

Once the human psyche achieved the level where man was able to acknowledge his existence apart from that of others and from nature, we experienced the loneliness of selfhood. We are now aware of our individual existence and this affords us innumerable opportunities for creative adventures. As we accentuate the self, we discover that we are no longer one with other humans or with nature. The struggle we experience in the process of self-actualization is a struggle to meet the human need to be one with reality. The Christian response to this struggle is the love of Jesus which demonstrates that the ambiguity of self-fulfillment is overcome in the realization of the love of God for all creation. The Christian woman brought to an awareness of death does not have to respond, "eat, drink and fornicate for tomorrow we die."

Rather, the *responsible woman* knows that she possesses certain talents or gifts which she must identify and put to use in the proclamation of the Good News. A suburban woman who wishes to move out of the mythical world and assume her place in the real world will, due to her previous conditioning, need to make a conscious effort to evaluate her lifestyle in the view of her understanding of the *responsible woman.* In most instances decisions will need to be made and goals established. Each woman is responsible for her own "Design for Living a Christian Life." We will enumerate some of the considerations which should go into the planning of such a design.

Will the Real Me Please Stand Up? The suburban woman has been conforming to role expectations for such a long period of time that she is liable to find herself drifting from one fad to another. It is crucial that we make decisions based on what *we* want to do, not on what others tell us is fashionable. Getting a job, full- or even part-time, is not what every woman wants to do. Nor is every woman capable of handling the physical and emotional demands of home and a job. Although many within the women's movement claim that they do not advocate that all women work, somehow the message has been translated that way by the time it reaches the suburbs.

So, too, with going to school, playing tennis, doing needlepoint, participating in a consciousness-raising group, learning Parent Effectiveness Training techniques, or joining a Pentecostal prayer group, all of which are fashionable activities for the suburban woman in the mid-1970s. New fads will develop as we grow bored with some of these alternatives, and those who are in the business of persuading us that their thing is *the* thing to be doing will find new activities to push. Unless we are fairly certain who the *real me* is, we will find ourselves continually following the crowd. One of the beauties of the freedom of the suburban woman is that she is free to choose how she wants to use her talents. We should not turn this opportunity into another ritual of conformity.

Dare to Dream Dreams or Have Visions. The prophet Joel promised that when the Spirit is among us the old will dare to dream dreams and the young will have visions. This power released by life in the Spirit enables us to imagine ourselves doing things that had never before seemed possible. Freedom in the Spirit allows us at age forty to dream of returning to school for that degree in art that we passed up twenty years ago.

The husband of one of the participants in the Ladies' Theology program thought women should spend their extra hours discovering what it means to *be* as opposed to finding meaning in what one is *doing*. The basis of his contention was that men have to work to support their families, and consequently men have come to find that the only way they achieve meaning in life is from what they *do*. Now that woman is free of many of the *doing* chores of family life, she should turn her energies to the topic of *being*, thereby helping both men and women appreciate that our whole value in life should not spring from a work-related situation. There is some merit to this suggestion, especially for those women who are inclined to be philosophical. Yet based on the list of activities and amount of time spent on these activities by the women I interviewed, I am inclined to think that most of us try desperately to avoid this type of thinking. Nor should the question of what it means *to be*, be addressed only by women.

We must also expand our vision to include larger amounts of time and space. Since we have not been conditioned to plan past the child-bearing years, we must begin to imagine ourselves as creative women when we are in our sixties and all our children live far away. We must overcome our tendency to consider our world as the universe. One point that came through very clear in interviewing suburban women was their inability to see themselves as part of a bigger kingdom than their own suburban milieu. The suburban woman who says that there are no differences between suburban women and other women demonstrates that she is unaware of what goes on outside her community.

Though we can not single-handedly solve all the vast crises of today's world, we are capable of developing an interest in social concerns. We should be addressing the problems of world hunger and of the energy crisis, not simply by eating less or turning off lights. Dare to imagine yourself at conference tables contributing well-thought out and valuable suggestions for possible solutions to these problems. Of course it would require a great deal of preparation on your part to qualify for such a role, but why have small visions, if one can achieve larger goals?

Follow Your Star. Needless to say, it is not enough to dream of returning to art school, or participating in a world conference on the food crisis. Nor is it enough to envision yourself a creative writer at age sixty-five or achieving whatever secret dream, large or small, you would like to accomplish. The Spirit is with us to help us dream dreams. He will also remain with us if we take constructive steps to follow through on the dreams He helps us dream. I would imagine that even He would eventually grow tired of staying around a group of Walter Mittys who engaged in outlandish daydreams simply for the enjoyment of daydreaming.

One advantage of the human being's ability to daydream is that it allows us to be open to future possibilities. But these future possibilities will become realities only if people are willing to work at making them come true. A woman who wants to develop her creative writing abilities must plan what steps she should take in order to achieve her dream. When I asked the women what talents they would like to develop there was a variety of interests indicated. However, aside from some art, guitar, sewing and tennis lessons, little was being done to ensure that these talents would ever be more than just a passing interest. And there was little indication that the lessons were part of a serious developmental plan.

The skill that the women seemed most interested in developing was their tennis ability, and many suburban women spend two and three hours a day perfecting their game. In the year which has passed since the initial interviews, however, some of the women who were most enthusiastic about tennis have grown bored with it and are looking for something else to do. Although they still enjoy a good game of tennis, they are no longer dedicating every minute of their free time to it.

Goal-setting and follow-up planning will not be easy for women who have been accustomed to fitting into the same mold as everyone else. This has required little effort on our part. It is difficult to determine who set the original mold, but it has never seemed that important to us. We simply went along with the rules of the game. If we determine to initiate new rules for ourselves we will find it necessary to give up our childlike self-image and address ourselves seriously to the question of what I want to do and what steps must I take in order to achieve that goal. We were once good at this. After all, we did decide that we wanted to marry and took the necessary steps to achieve that goal. That, of course, is a more natural goal and was probably more easily achieved than some of our present dreams. In every instance, however, dreams do not become realities unless we make them so.

Respect Your Husbands. Marabel Morgan has advocated that we accept, admire, adapt to and appreciate our husbands. Yet some of the advice she and Helen Andelin are passing out leads me to maintain that the most important attitude the *responsible woman* should have toward her husband, in addition to love, is respect. When we married fifteen, twenty, or thirty years ago we had a dream of a house in the suburbs and saw our role as heart of the home with our place in the home. Our husbands shared that dream with us. While they have been busily involved in furthering their careers and we have been involved in caring for children, our understanding of the reality of that dream world has changed.

Perhaps you are fortunate enough to have a husband who has been observant of this change; but, based on what I hear from women in the Ladies' Theology program and those who come to the School for New Learning, it appears that while women are living with the reality of their opportunities for freedom, their husbands have, in effect, found themselves less free. Getting ahead in the world has made such demands on their time that they begin to feel caged in by the time they reach forty. No wonder it comes as a surprise to them when their wives inform them they are considering going back to school or work to fill up their free time, particularly if communication between the couple has been poor. A husband is apt to react negatively to such a suggestion; even more so if he is feeling caught up in the white, middle-age, middle-class male syndrome at work where affirmative action programs seem to be shattering his dreams.

Respect for our husbands demands that we sincerely attempt to reestablish communications where they have broken down, specifically on the issue of the woman's role. With our husbands we form the smallest of communities, the place where, as Rollo May indicates, we should be able to "depend upon my fellows for support." At the same time, the intimacy of the everyday community of husband and wife requires tenderness and care if it is to overcome the ambiguity of all human community. With our vision of romantic love at the time of marriage, we naively thought that things would be perfect, at least "for us," even when we saw it was not always so with others. We failed to appreciate the amount of effort that must be given to developing true communion. As a result, most married couples do not find the marital situation the place where they can accept their loneliness, rather they seem to experience even greater loneliness.

A woman who is in the process of reevaluating her lifestyle must remember that she is part of this community and, if her husband is not yet at the point of understanding the need for this reevaluation, she must work at including him in the process. So many women complain that "My husband doesn't want me to work," or "I'd love to go to school, but my husband won't let me." It is becoming apparent that many women are using the "my husband" excuse as a way of holding firm to their child-like image. Of course, many husbands will react negatively to an entirely new idea. It does not mean that they will remain completely close-minded on the subject if it is reasonably presented.

One woman told me that her husband would not allow her to engage in more than a minimal number of activities outside the home. He felt, according to her, that a mother should always be at home with the children. On the other hand, he told me that he felt it would be good for her to get some part-time job outside the home. She was, in his opinion, too attached to the home and kids and it would be good for her to have some outside interest. Obviously she and her husband have not discussed this issue at much length.

Another woman who had been turned on by a feminist speaker was convinced that the only way for her to become self-fulfilled was to divorce her husband. Before taking this drastic step, however, she was going to get her degree so she would not have to be financially dependent upon him. When confronted with the realization that she was a self, this woman, who had obviously resented living in the shadow of her successful husband, was determined not only to achieve her human potential, but also to destroy what little communion she shared with this man. She saw no middle path.

Few humans are very good at the art of loving, yet all of us, men and women alike, desperately want to love and be loved. After ten years or more of marriage we have established patterns of relating to our spouse which can be changed only with great effort. Though our marital relationship is probably not what we had hoped it to be, we adopt a fatalistic attitude and maintain, "Well, at least it's better than a lot of others around here." We drift along, not growing together, but growing apart. The woman's realization that she must reevaluate her lifestyle could present a couple with an opportunity to reevaluate their life together and, thus, be a contributing factor to improving their relationship. Though most men are not as able to express their dependency needs, there is just as great a desire on their part to find happiness within marriage as there is for the woman. The *responsible woman* should be ready to offer her husband a chance to grow, too.

But she should be prepared for her husband to take her up on the offer. It is questionable how responsive many feminist women would be to overnight acceptance of equality of the sexes. An adult relationship, and especially in a marriage, demands a great deal of giving on the part of both partners. It is impossible for a woman to give of herself unless she has first acquired an understanding of who she is and what she has to give. It is mandatory that she recognize the importance of her sexuality and the need to give freely of herself in this aspect of her marital relationship. Marabel Morgan's advice on recognizing the importance of sex as a comfort to the male should be extended to an admission that it is of equal importance to a female.

Once "nice girls" were taught that sex was not to be enjoyed, but if we have difficulty in admitting the importance of sexual fulfillment in our lives we will be certain to never achieve the full enjoyment of an adult marital relationship. Widespread use of the Pill has forced many individuals to an uncomfortable confrontation with their true feelings about their sexuality. The possibility of sexual relations at any time without the fear of pregnancy places demands on people to be honest in evaluating their own sexual powers and desires.

The difficulty I have with Morgan's heavy emphasis on a woman's life centering around being a mistress to her husband springs from the fact that I find her suggestions manipulative. They fail to recognize that it is important for a man and woman to relate on many other levels. It *is* fun to seduce your husband. But if you and he are not *both* helping each other discover and develop the talents which will make your family a Christian community and help you proclaim the Good News in joy and fellowship, then all the seduction routines in the world are worthless.

Rejoice. When my daughter, Elizabeth, was three or four years old, there was a song she used to sing. It was her theme song in those days. It went something like this:

Be Happy! / Be Happy! / Be Happy All Day Long!
Be Happy! / Be Happy! / And Sing Your Happy Song!

It was really quite an appropriate song for her in those days, and even though three years of school seemed to have disciplined some of the natural joyfulness out of her, at age eight she still seems to know how to enjoy life. I imagine we must all have been like that at some time in our lives; and I think this is what the celebration of the Good News is all about. In spite of the fact that we are much more aware than a little girl of all kinds of reasons to be unhappy, we still should be happy.

I am not advocating a naive approach to reality, or denying that many people have great crosses to bear. Rather, I am suggesting that, as Christians, we have an obligation to teach others, by our example, that life is still worth living. We have to learn to sing the Happy Song in such a manner that our singing will be as appealing as that of a three-year-old.

To the suburban woman faced with the dilemma of changing roles, the prospect of ever being really happy often seems quite remote. We seriously accept the challenge of being Supermoms and sometimes it works; but all too often it seems that we have failed. So many women I deal with have staked so much of their happiness on the success of their children that they spend most of their time worrying about all the problems facing young people today. There is no time for rejoicing for them. Then if the children fail to measure up to the mother's expectation there are always plenty of amateur psychologists around to put the whole blame on Mom.

This placing of our hopes for success on the achievements of our children became apparent to me when my eldest daughter was about six years old. One day as I was doing the dishes—I can recall the scene vividly— I was relieving the monotony of that task by daydreaming. I was daydreaming about how Laura was going to meet and marry the young son of a famous family. Suddenly, in the midst of my dishwashing I came back to reality with a thud: a thud and the scary feeling that something was not quite right. Here I was, only twenty-eight-years old; and my thoughts of what I would accomplish in life were centering around who my six-year-old would marry. I must admit that was the first in a series of events which brought me to an understanding that my original marital vow to never leave the home needed rethinking.

I was fortunate in having a doctor who advised me at the time of the birth of my first child to relax and enjoy her. "She will grow up all too soon." Obviously I do not have a perfect record of enjoying every moment of child-rearing. However, his words helped me feel I did not have to run to Doctor Spock or every article on child-rearing available. I still cannot predict what the future holds for my children, but I have enjoyed them thus far. I find myself wanting to say to a mother who is concerned that her first-grader is not a top reader, "Relax," but when she says, "Well, I do want him to get a good job," I don't know how to respond.

The *responsible woman* going about a plan for a design of Christian living must be sure to include the need for a sense of humor. At times the only thing that will keep even a spark of that sense of humor alive is her faith in the Good News, but a spark is enough. If it is joined by other sparks it might even grow back into a flame.

Have Courage. One reason many women who are seriously rethinking their lifestyles have so little time for rejoicing is that they are faced with the reality of their fears. As we observed earlier, social myths die hard, and those who choose to engage in the murder often risk being ostracized. There is a security in doing the task assigned to us by society. If we openly respond to new opportunities for freedom and move away from these clearly defined roles, we run the risk of any pioneer. We have no maps to follow. We must take chances. We might even fail. Who knows what will happen if we spend time and money on art lessons and it turns out we do not have the talent we thought we had? What guarantee do we have that if we really commit ourselves to serious work on a volunteer project, we might be working on it the day the school calls to tell us our child is sick and needs us? How can we be sure that our husband will eventually be understanding of our need to expand our horizons? The answer to all of these questions is we cannot be sure what will happen. As Christian women, we do have the security of knowing that the risks are worth it, if, in the long run we are contributing to the spread of the Good News. Even our failures are acceptable to God. What is not acceptable is turning away from an opportunity to follow Jesus. Those opportunities are not always as clearly defined as they were to the Rich Young Man, but the opportunities to use our freedoms are chances we may never have again. As one woman I interviewed summed it up:

Opportunities, that's what I think is our greatest advantage. They are ours if we're willing to pursue them. We have the opportunity to stay at home and devote ourselves to the community; or we are free to go to work or go to school. That doesn't mean we take advantage of them. I'm just not sure what's going to happen if we sit by and never take advantage of any of these chances. I guess that could be one of the disadvantages for us as we get older . . . if we haven't done anything we could be pretty lonely.

Support Each Other. This final point which a *responsible woman* should bear in mind as she sets out to prepare her design is one of the most important and most difficult for suburban women. Sisterhood, a word used by the women's movement to symbolize their support of each other in the struggle for equality is a word which has been used frequently in circles of both Christian and Jewish women. Unfortunately, as a rabbi observed, "The Sisterhood in our community addresses itself solely to social events. We have tried to get the women interested in other things, but it never seems to work." His lament sounded familiar to me as I have often heard the same comments from Catholic priests and Protestant ministers. Women's groups in most local churches do allow opportunities for neighboring and other social functions, but when they move into more serious areas their success record is low. This is one reason why the response to the Ladies' Theology Program was so surprising.

Even in the theology program the women have been unable to be really supportive of each other in the area of changing lifestyles. In our parish, the women are famous for their willingness to help out in an emergency. Whenever a family is in need of support during a time of illness or death, helping hands abound. As the number of widows increase, there is a group offering support based on their own experiences.

Yet, when it comes to a woman not conforming to the image of what is expected of her, the supporting hands are few and far between. This is not a situation unique to our community; nor is it unique among women. The human tendency to feel threatened by someone who is doing something "different," especially if that something different seems exciting or attractive, seems to be widespread.

I was on a panel at Mundelein College when one of the faculty members, a feminist, pronounced, "The problem is that we are at war; and we are sleeping with the enemy." "Not so," I retorted, "the enemy for most women is other women." My views were confirmed by a female manager from a large corporation who maintains that the women who are moving up in management are having their biggest difficulties in dealing with the petty jealousies of other women.

A woman I work with is extremely well-organized.

She seems to have magical powers which allow her to accomplish what it takes most other people three times the amount of time and energy to achieve. She does all the things she does because, as she says, "I enjoy it." This seems a perfectly legitimate reason for her behavior. What she does, she does well; and at the same time she appears to manage a family of involved and interesting young people. Yet, she feels strong vibrations of disapproval from many women, some of whom she considers friends, when she accomplishes another "impossible" task. "Why are you bothering to do that?" they will say. "You do so much already." Needless to say, she finds this deflating. How much better she would feel if they'd say, "It's really wonderful you are able to do that."

The radical feminists maintain that the reason women in our situations cannot support each other is that we are vying for masculine attention. The backbiting and complaining which goes on in suburban women's organizations proves that we are not capable of working together for a common cause. That is not true, according to the feminists: in their groups they are not interested in male reaction. Again, I disagree. My experiences with women from feminist groups does not bear out their claim that they are such great supporters of each other. I do agree that suburban women do not support each other. The cause for this, though, I attribute to the frustration they are experiencing in their mythical world; and *frustrated* women cannot support each other. The *responsible woman,* who sees herself as a member of a Christian community, must take seriously the command to "love one another," and love includes support.

6

The Community
Responds to Women

One popular thesis on the response of
the Christian churches to the changing role of women
expresses the sentiment that once again the churches
have missed the boat. Emancipation for women is a
reality and not only did the churches have nothing to
do with it, they are trying to pretend it never occurred.
The secular world has scored again, and there is nothing left for the Church to do.

What a thesis such as this neglects to recognize is that
true emancipation for women is far from a reality. The
theory of equality of the sexes is in most instances just
that, a theory. Women in an increasing number of
countries have received the right to vote. We in America have, as the advertisement tells us, "come a long
way" since Grandma's day; but, as our study of the
suburban woman indicates, although opportunities for
freedom might be present, the majority are never
acted upon. There are also increasing signs of polarization between the sexes; the feminists maintain that they

must withdraw to the fringes of our society and work out a woman's culture before they will be able to work with men. Equally destructive ideas on the relationship between the sexes are developing among males. Many have grudgingly given in at work to the demands of women under the pressure of affirmative action programs, but outside of the work environment they are more hostile to women than they had previously been.

Jane Trahey, president of her own advertising agency and a Mundelein College alumna, gave a presentation at a Woman's Day program at the school in the fall of 1974. The theme of her presentation was "Baby, You've Got a Long Way to Go." Ms. Trahey's multi-media presentation depicted the song, film and commercial treatment of women twenty-five years ago, and analyzed how the role of woman was portrayed at that time. Projecting ahead to a similar undertaking in the year 2000 A.D; she questioned how much progress has been achieved in the changing of woman's image. Songs, movies, television commercials, and the majority of daytime television programming continue to portray the stereotypical image of woman. Trahey's presentation disturbed those in the audience who felt women were making great strides toward equality. Even more disturbing were her statistics on women's achievements in the world of business. "One out of 5,000 retail stores in the United States has a woman president. Two women head their own advertising firms, out of a total of 6,000 agencies." Her conclusion was that until we are able to operate from a "position where we make the decisions about what women's image in the media should be,"[1] we will continue to be plagued with the view of woman as either the dumb blonde or a sex symbol.

My concern, and one which I think is a clear example of where the Christian churches have a contribution to make, centers around her statement "about what women's image in the media should be." If the women who eventually move into positions of power in the advertising and media world are women who have been turned off by the patriarchal society and have a gripe with the entire male world, polarization will increase even more. Unfortunately, the suburban woman who sits passively by and fails to present her daughters with workable role models for a fulfilling life is contributing to the possible alienated feelings of a future woman in the advertising field.

Thus we would be naive to assume that there is nothing left for the churches to do in helping women achieve equality and reducing the tensions which presently exist between the sexes. The problem of sexual polorization is of equal importance to that of racial conflict, war, and poverty. True, most churches have not begun to recognize the critical nature of the polarization; but that does not mean there is nothing they can and should do. This is especially true in a local church which adopts a vision similar to the one we have outlined. How can a community possibly proclaim the Good News in celebration and fellowship when half the congregation has hostile feelings toward the other half? And the fact that there are few ardent feminists in most suburban churches does not mean there is no hostility. Once again the listening pastoral theologian should pick up loud and clear signals of the difficulties both men and women are having coping with woman's changing role.

The question, of course, arises concerning where a local church should begin. Indeed, how can a local community, where the women seem uninterested in the issue of equality among the sexes, even begin to approach the problem of sexual polarization? In today's local suburban church, the responsibility for exercising leadership on this issue rests, for the most part, with the clergy. Whether they want to accept this responsibility of leadership or not, the fact still remains that most of the church membership still looks to the clergyman for spiritual guidance. Though church boards and church councils are increasing in many congregations, and in some denominations they even exercise the power to remove a pastor, the clergy bear the responsibility of prodding the congregation to work at living up to its vision.

This is not an easy task, especially since most of the clergy have the same cultural conditioning as the members of the congregation. It is difficult for a cleric, who in most instances is a male, to be attuned to the complexity of the issue directly facing the women within the congregation. Yet he has the responsibility to minister to all the members of the community, and women generally make up at least half that membership.

According to the women I surveyed, the parish priest was doing "as good a job as any other male around here" at trying to understand the women of the community. The priests also felt they were trying, though one admitted, "It's really a hard task for any man to try to understand a woman, so I'm not sure how successful our efforts are." Though I believe many clergymen are trying to be responsive to the needs of women it is unacceptable for them to maintain that "women are difficult to understand, thus it is highly improbable that a male cleric has much to offer toward solving woman's dilemma."

The cleric must familiarize himself with the dilemma of the suburban woman and begin to explore the implications of what he observes with the members of the community. This will increase both his and their understanding of the issue. As we observed earlier, a clergyman who has developed an image of the changing woman based on readings or associations with members of feminist organizations is going to meet with fierce opposition if he begins to promote these ideas in a suburban community. This does not, however, mean that he should ignore the needs of the women within the congregation he is serving. One way to gain insight into these needs is to begin to discuss the issue, and then be prepared to listen, as Shea says, not only to what is said, but also to what is left unsaid.

Although it is true that cultural conditioning makes it difficult for a male cleric to move with ease on the issue of woman's place, his role as spiritual leader of the community dictates that he continually remind the congregation of the implications of the Christian message for their daily lives. He must constantly present the challenge to the people to respond to the Good News. In the case of the suburban woman, he must be willing to risk challenging her to give up her pseudo-innocence. Behavior which lacks direction should be questioned, even if that behavior is serving a need of the church.

Needless to say, it would be impossible for a clergyman to accomplish this on his own. Though it is his responsibility to be aware of the situation and to challenge and support, the wise minister marshals all the help he can in carrying out these functions. The local church is a Spirit-filled community where the members are free, as Rollo May maintains, to "depend upon my fellows to support me . . . the source of my physical courage in that knowing I can depend on others, I guarantee that they also can depend on me." It is within the framework of such a community concept that the minister can challenge women to be supportive of each other.

The natural place to begin is with the various women's groups that presently exist within a congregation. Though some of these organizations are beginning to expand their functions from strictly social to some service-oriented activities there is room, as one priest put it "for them to become more conscious of the needs of others both within our community and in the other parts of the metropolitan area." Generally the minister performs some form of an advisory role to these groups, and if he is seriously concerned about the dilemma of the suburban woman, he should suggest ways in which the women could become more conscious of the opportunities in their lives. He should also encourage them to put their freedom to constructive use.

One priest mentioned to me that he felt the women of the community were overinvolved in the lives of their children. They were, in his opinion, putting too much pressure on the children to succeed, in everything from winning sporting events to turning junior high plays into Broadway productions. Such an observation is undoubtedly true: yet these women, who have been conditioned to be Supermoms, are not conscious of how they are affecting their children with this behavior. A minister who observes this behavior should be willing to investigate its cause and discuss his insights with the community. Within the framework of a woman's group he could begin to guide their attention to issues such as these which are obvious obstacles to their ability to proclaim the Good News in celebration and fellowship.

The minister must be willing to challenge the men and women within the congregation to face the problem of polarization. All attempts at building community which ignore this underlying problem are bound to fail. The increased emphasis on this polarization in situations not related to the church cause tensions for the members that are bound to cause repercussions as a congregation goes about trying to define its Christian mission. Women, as our survey indicated, presently do most of the work within our parish, but the clergy are anxious to involve the men more. As a result they are wary of involving women too heavily in additional tasks. At Mary, Seat of Wisdom, the priests are concerned that the impetus to work out a theological vision begun at the Mission will receive more follow-through attention from the women than the men. They are fearful of reverse sexism.

Though this is a legitimate fear, there has not been a visible concern on their part about the lack of female participation in the new roles open to lay people in the celebration of the liturgy. It is now possible within the Catholic Church for lay people to function as lectors, commentators and lay ministers of communion at liturgical functions. For many years the roles of commentator and lector were filled only by men. Since permission was granted for women to perform these roles there have been only a few women, mostly teenage girls serving in these capacities. One of the priests mentioned that he would like to see more women in these roles. The reason they had not encouraged it sooner he said was, "We were afraid that women sitting out in the congregation would be jealous that a particular woman was up there and they were not." If a supposedly open-minded priest, who is trying to be attuned to the changing role of women, says this without any consciousness then my response would be "Why do you think only women would react this way?" It is obvious that we do have a long way to go. Until there are an equal number of men and women performing all these roles a congregation cannot be satisfied that its members are being represented in the celebration of the Eucharist.

The blame for this unequal representation does not rest entirely on the clergy. Women have not offered their services as lectors and commentators. Given our understanding of the lack of confidence among women, however, it is obvious they need additional encouragement to respond to a request for new participants. In the case of lay ministers of communion these people are asked to assume the role, and, from the beginning, there has been an unequal representation. Though there has been an increase in the percentage of women each year, a number of these are nuns and persons connected with the school. Yet in all instances of lay participation Mary, Seat of Wisdom Parish has one of the best records among the parishes in the Catholic archdiocese for including women. Breaking down taboos in the minds of both men and women about women performing liturgical functions is a difficult task. Nevertheless it must be accomplished if the local church is to witness to the dangers of polarization.

A large obstacle to accepting a changing role for women in the local church springs from a failure to communicate to the laity a theology of woman. As Nancy Hardesty pointed out to me, "If you have spent twenty-five or more years of your life being the submissive woman because you believed God created woman subordinate to man, it can be devastating to have someone raise questions about that interpretation of God's plan." Acceptance of a view of *responsible woman* will be possible for many women, and men, only after a sufficient period of time has been allowed for them to become familiar with a new theological view. It will come more quickly if they join in the formulation of such a view by contributing their own experiences and being encouraged to fit them into a Christian framework.

As the members of the community contribute their experiences, it will become obvious that both men and women need support as they attempt to cope with the tension of role definitions. Some husbands are perhaps unjustly accused of interfering with their wives' attempts at self-actualization, but many suburban males are quite honestly confused by the changing role situation and react by being defensive. They find their masculinity being questioned and are then confronted with a need to define masculinity. The suburban woman needs support if she is to break out of her mythical prison. The suburban man needs to understand that he has been imprisoned also, and that allowing his wife to develop her talents is no threat to him. The suburban couple need encouragement to have faith in themselves and in their love for each other.

In effect what is needed in most suburban churches is a form of consciousness-raising for both the men and women of the parish; a consciousness-raising which allows them to appreciate the wonder of the Good News and supports them as they attempt to deal with their fear of change. If the members of a local church view themselves as participants in a Spirit-filled community, they may acquire the moral courage to begin to fight the polarization of the sexes both in the Church and in the other environments in which they live and work.

This is the challenge and the opportunity that is present in a local church. The challenge is to work out, in a supportive and challenging community, their own difficulties regarding the polarization of the sexes. If this is achieved then as the community proclaims the Good News in celebration and fellowship, it will be witnessing to the rest of the world the possibility of eventually eliminating the tension between the sexes. It will demonstrate *in reality* an answer to the myth of woman's place. An impossible dream? We have the Spirit in our midst to help us dream and the Lord's promise that He would be always with us.

7
Women in Ministry

I am certain that there will come a day when the heavy emotional investment in keeping the clergy male will fade away and women will assume ordained ministerial roles in the majority of churches. This will probably happen around the same time that women begin, in large numbers, to assume other leadership roles in our society. I agree with Krister Stendahl that once we admit that God did not create woman inferior to man we can no longer maintain a theological position that keeps women from ordination.[1]

Also I have come now to feel that the issue of women's ordination *is* relevant. Scanzoni and Hardesty argue convincingly that a priesthood of believers is the model for the future; they maintain that Luther made the same claim four hundred years ago. Their emphasis on the advantages of ordination both for the person wishing to perform a leadership role in the church and for those to whom they minister, seems valid to me. For the former, ordination is a guarantee of support from the church. For the latter it provides more ministers than would be possible if we limit the ministry to only half the human race.[2]

Having reviewed the history of women since the suffragette days of the nineteenth century, I will not predict that this will happen in the immediate future. It does not seem that the rights women have acquired in the last decade will be given up, but circumstances could alter the situation and find women returning to the home. In any case theological arguments against ordination for women will still have no foundation.

The real issue that must be faced for the churches today and even when women are routinely accepted for ordination is: what meaning does this have for the women who are not ordained? Men have been participating in the priesthood for almost two thousand years and the male who is not ordained still has no better understanding of his role as a Christian than does a woman. So, although I advocate and will welcome ordination of women in all denominations, I would like to see more emphasis placed on other types of ministerial functions which women could perform without being officially ordained.

As our survey indicates, women are performing many functions within the church which were considered ecclesiastical tasks in the early church. Religious education is a task in many local churches that is almost exclusively under the direction of women. As in the biblical church, these women are guardians of the tradition and they engage in pastoral-ethical instruction. (Rom. 12:17). In the New Testament this was a special ministry included by Paul along with the role of apostle and prophet as one of the three positions of the church.

Religious education is a task that women have performed well. In many Protestant denominations it is acknowledged as the special ministry of women. However, there is still a lack of appreciation of the depth of knowledge and preparatory training a religious educator should have. Many times it is a volunteer function, sometimes performed under the supervision of a specialist, but often presided over by a person of good will. Given the interest of many women in doing something worthwhile with their free time, it seems that more attention should be paid to the ministerial aspects of this role. Ministry requires a good deal more than dedication and is also more rewarding than teaching religious education. Ministry requires preparation, commitment, and prayerlife, all of which many religious educators are currently doing. However, official recognition of this role by the educators and by the remainder of the community would ensure a greater feeling of support for the efforts these women are making.

Another important function of the New Testament community was that of pastoral care. This referred to the service function performed by the original followers of Jesus. All the missionary and apostolic work of an apostle was a function of service (Acts 20:24; 21:19; Rom 11:13; 1 Cor. 3:5) and the Christian community was subject to Christ through the service of the Apostles and disciples who were "fellow workers in your joy; for in faith you stand" (2 Cor. 1:24).

In addition to this function of pastoral care which was a function of the offical ministry, there was a ministry of service which saw to the sick and needy among the brethren (Acts 6:1-6), and was also performed by the women of the community (I Tim. 5:3-16). The challenge to the contemporary local church is to identify those functions presently performed by women which fall into this category as well as designating possible new areas of service which would make use of the immense variety of talents present in a particular local community.

The contemporary suburban woman who is aware of her opportunities for freedom and is seeking to design a plan for a Christian life might choose to become more actively involved in the ministerial aspects of the church if she could be challenged to decide what services she could offer and how these are related to the mission of the Church.

One complaint a parish priest had about the Ladies' Theology Program was that it was a passive activity for the participants. Although for some women it pointed the way to new directions for their lives, for the majority it was a passive acquisition of knowledge. There has been little, if any, visible effect on the life of the community as a result of a large number of the members attending this program.

What I would propose as a possible approach to determining the wealth of potential ministerial talents available among the women of a local church, is the inauguration of a program, similar to the Ladies' Theology Program, but smaller in size. In such a program women could begin to explore the needs of the local church, if it is to live up to its vision, and at the same time they could begin to discover the various resources they have which could meet these needs. From such a program these women who would like to be more actively involved in the ministerial aspects of the church could design a plan for how they would implement their findings.

This would not be an attempt to revive or revitalize a dying Ladies' Auxiliary, but a whole new concept of attempting to allow the women of the parish to develop and use their talents in a way that would be rewarding and meaningful for them. It would not be a busy-work endeavor, but a serious program of offering service and commitment to a role in the church. It might require additional education to equip women with the knowledge and skills they need to perform certain ministerial tasks, both in the local community and in the world outside the church.

If a local church is to be *a Spirit-filled community which knows of God's plan of salvation through Jesus and proclaims it in celebration and fellowship,* it is going to require the dedication of many more people than the present number of ordained ministers. The suburban woman who is a member of a Christian community will, in many instances, be happy to give her time to serving the community. What I am advocating is that she be challenged to realize the value of her time and commitment by identifying it as a form of ministry.

These are some brief exploratory thoughts on how the needs of the suburban woman and the needs of the local church might be joined in a variety of serious ministerial endeavors. Each local church will have differing needs and talents, but all would undoubtedly benefit from challenging the women of the community to use their buried talents whenever possible in the proclamation of the Good News.

The role of the suburban woman is changing, in her home, in the world and in the church. The possibilities are there for her to enrich herself, her home, her world and her church. The task will not be an easy one. Let us hope that the faith of the *responsible woman* will sustain her as she explores uncharted paths.

8
Our Time Is Now

The theme for one year of the Ladies' Theology Program was "Thank God Our Time is Now." This phrase from Christopher Fry's *Sleep of Prisoners,* decorated the cover of the packets of reading material given to each participant and was proclaimed on a large banner displayed each time the group gathered.

There were some within the group who had difficulty accepting this slogan since they felt life had been so much better in the good old days when there were strict guidelines for moral behavior. We knew that by following these guidelines we would be assured of salvation. How could anyone be thankful that we were living in times of such enormous upheaval, not only in the secular world, but even within the churches?

The upheaval continues six years after the year of being thankful our time is now, and undoubtedly will continue for a considerable period of time. Yet, even as the upheaval continues, the reasons for being thankful also continue. In the midst of the upheaval it is becoming more and more apparent that people are searching for a sense of meaning in their lives. As Fry also observes, either consciously or unconsciously our searching indicates that "The enterprise is exploration unto God."

And it is exploration unto God which is the motivating factor behind any attempt to practice the art of pastoral theology. The identification of the paradigmatic experience, the illumination of this experience by setting it within the framework of the Christian tradition, and the enumeration of strategies for action that flow from the merger of experience and tradition are all part of the art which Shea defines as "the primordial act of interpreting the Really Real and trying to live in communion with it."[1]

The determination that the paradigmatic experience of suburban woman is in increased opportunities for freedom and the placing of her situation within the context of her membership in a local church community has suggested certain strategies of action. There are undoubtedly other experiences and other symbols from the tradition which would suggest still other strategies for action.

The primary difference between the pastoral theology of fifty years ago and pastoral theology today is that we will no longer be able to contain within the pages of any one book, no matter how big, the definitive answer to exactly what a suburban woman must do if she wants assurance of salvation. Pastoral theology is a process and, as a process it must continually reexamine the principles it uncovers in attempting to interpret the Really Real. The pastoral theologian, whether clerical or lay, must be constantly open to the possibility of new insights which could suggest different interpretations.

We have attempted in this book to explore a possible approach to a pastoral theology for suburban women. The image of the Christian woman as a *responsible woman,* responding to the call of Christ as she encounters new opportunities for freedom, leads to the necessity of each woman working out her own design for living a Christian life. But an understanding of the social nature of humans makes us realize that it is only within the framework of a community that a woman will be able to successfully design and implement her program.

The challenge that is present for the Christian churches in the contemporary polarization of the sexes is one which cannot continue to go unheeded. It is the responsibility of the pastoral theologian and of lay women and men to articulate the problems which this polarization is causing. During one week while I was writing this book I learned of five marriages within our parish community which had broken up. For a parish of just under two thousand families this might not seem like a large number. However, these are five that I heard of. They are people whom I know. They are all people who at one time or other have been active within the parish community. Although I am not familiar enough with any of these couples to know why their marriages failed, it is obvious that many people in the suburbs are suffering in their marital relationships. A good deal of this suffering flows from the increased polarization of the sexes, and until the churches begin to understand this there are going to be more and more failed marriages. Twenty-four children, in addition to the ten adults, are involved in what is undoubtedly a distressing situation. It would probably be quite difficult for most of them to proclaim "Thank God Our Time Is Now."

Yet the proportions of the problems which are present in family life in a suburban setting often appear so overwhelming that the priest or minister considers himself lucky if he is able to apply a Band-Aid here or there and rarely has time to devote to contemplating possible preventive measures. But a family held together with Band-Aids will, in most instances, be unable to join in the proclamation of the Good News in celebration and fellowship.

Given the breadth of the problem and the scarity of clergy in many suburban churches, it seems that clergy and laity will need to pool their talents if they are to be successful in the development of a pastoral theology. This will necessitate setting up some process which will allow the laity and clergy to interact on topics of major importance within the community. Someone at the beginning, probably the clergy, should initiate a program which will allow for a free exchange of ideas. It will not be enough to sit back and wait for awareness to surface among all the members of the community. There are people in all suburban churches right now who are willing, and with some encouragement would undoubtedly be able to join with the clergy in such an enterprise. Though Shea's description of the pastoral theologian refers to the minister, it could as easily apply to any group which is attempting to arrive at a common consciousness of the meaning and responsibility of the Christian community.

The task of such a group would be "exploration unto God" in which guidelines for a Christian life could be developed. These guidelines would not have the authoritarian force of the guidelines for moral behavior from previous times. However, if they are drawn up as a result of a merging of experience and the Christian tradition they will have a force far more attractive than a group of rules and regulations. If they are the result of the creative aspects of the group, they should offer an opportunity to others to sincerely feel, *thank God, our time is now.*

Notes

CHAPTER 1. INTRODUCTION

1. Marabel Morgan, *The Total Woman* (Old Tappan, New Jersey: Fleming H. Revell Company, 1973).
2. Helen B. Andelin, *Fascinating Womanhood* (New York: Bantam, 1975).
3. Mary Daly, *Beyond God the Father: Toward a Woman's Liberation* (Boston: Beacon Press, 1973).
4. Bernard Lonergan, S. J., *Method in Theology* (New York: Herder & Herder, 1972), p. 366.
5. See *The Pastoral Mission of the Church, Concilium: Theology in the Age of Renewal*, ed. by Karl Rahner and Heinz Schuster (Glen Rock, New Jersey: Paulist Press, 1965) vol. III; Frederick Schulze, *A Manual of Pastoral Theology: A Practical Guide for Ecclesiastical Students and Newly Ordained Priests* (St. Louis: B. Herder Book Co., 1944); Henry Davis, S. J., *Moral and Pastoral Theology: A Summary* (New York: Sheed and Ward, 1952).
6. H. Richard Niebuhr, *The Purpose of the Church and Its Ministry: Reflections on the Aims of Theological Education* (New York: Harper & Brothers, 1956), especially chapters 2 and 3.
7. John Shea, "An Approach to Pastoral Theology," in *Chicago Studies*, XII (Spring, 1973), pp. 20–21.
8. Langdon Gilkey maintained when teaching a course at the University of Chicago in the late 1960s on The Development of Liberal and Contemporary Theology, that the Roman Church is

trying to do in ten years what Protestants have been talking about for 150 years. With this in mind, it is interesting to view the ideas of Friedrich Schleiermacher on "practical theology," the crown of theological study. See especially *Brief Outline on the Study of Theology*, translated by Terrence N. Tice (Richmond: John Knox Press, 1966). Here Schleiermacher sees practical theology as a "kind of technology which in combining all the different branches of theology together" aids in the leadership of the Christian Church in its task of holding the various concerns of the Church together and building on them in a comprehensive and concentrated way. (pp. 125–156).

9. Shea, op. cit., p. 20.

CHAPTER 2. THE MYTHICAL WORLD OF THE SUBURBAN WOMEN

1. Betty Friedan, *The Feminine Mystique* (New York: Dell, 1963).
2. See *The Woman in the Modern World*, ed. by the Monks of Soloesmes (Boston: The Daughters of St. Paul, 1959).
3. Helen S. Astin, *The Woman Doctorate in America* (New York: The Russell Sage Foundation, 1969), p. 5.
4. Walter J. Imbiorski, ed., *The Basic Cana Manual* (Chicago: Delaney Publications, 1957), p. 79.
5. Ella May Miller, *A Woman in Her Home* (Chicago: Moody Press, 1968), p. 8.
6. John T. Durkin and Mary G. Durkin, "Preliminary Study of Problems of Working Wives" (Report prepared for the Cana Conference of Chicago, September, 1964).
7. Walter J. Imbiorski and John L. Thomas, *Beginning Your Marriage* (Chicago: Delaney Publications, 1966), p. 49. Emphasis mine.
8. Letha Scanzoni and Nancy Hardesty, *All We're Meant To Be* (Waco, Texas: Word Books, 1974), p. 170.
9. Elizabeth Janeway, *Man's World, Woman's Place: A Study in Social Mythology* (New York: Dell, 1971), p. 10.

CHAPTER 3. WOMEN ENCOUNTER FREEDOM

1. Emily James Putnam, *The Lady: Studies of Certain Significant Phases of Her History* (New York: Putnam's, 1910; reprint edition, Chicago: University of Chicago Press, 1969), pp. xxvii, xxxiii.
2. Helena Lopata, *Occupation: Housewife* (New York: Oxford University Press, 1971), p. 371.
3. Ibid., pp. 371–2.
4. Jane Jaffee Young, "Husband Dumping," from *The Village Voice*, February 24, 1975, p. 7.

5. Andelin, op. cit.
6. Morgan, op. cit.
7. Ibid, p. 80.
8. Rollo May, *Power and Innocence: A Search for the Sources of Violence* (New York: Norton, 1972).

CHAPTER 4. WOMAN IN THE LOCAL CHURCH

1. Cf. Scanzoni and Hardesty, op. cit.; Krister Stendahl, *The Bible and the Role of Women: A Case Study in Hermeneutics* (Philadelphia: Fortress Press, 1966).
2. Colin W. Williams, *New Directions in Theology Today*, Volume IV, "The Church" (Philadelphia: Westminster Press, 1958), p. 154.
3. Lopata, op. cit.
4. Paul Tillich, *Systematic Theology*, III (Chicago: University of Chicago Press, 1963), p. 166.
5. John Shea, "Theological Vision and the Local Church" (paper presented at meeting of group of Chicago priests, 1971), p. 8.
6. Ibid.
7. Robert Johann, *Building the Human* (New York: Herder & Herder, 1968), p. 82.
8. May, op. cit.
9. Tillich, op. cit.
10. Gregory Baum, *Man Becoming: God in Secular Experiences* (New York: Herder & Herder, 1970), p. 64.
11. Karl Rahner, *Theology of Pastoral Action*, transl. by W. J. O'Hara (New York: Herder & Herder, 1968), pp. 26–27.
12. Martin E. Marty, *A Short History of Christianity* (Cleveland: World Publishing Co., 1959), p. 184.

CHAPTER 5. WOMEN RESPOND TO FREEDOM

1. Andelin, op. cit.
2. H. Richard Niebuhr, *The Responsible Self: An Essay in Christian Moral Philosophy* (New York: Harper & Row, 1963), p. 162.
3. For a discussion of the various structures of existence associated with the evolving psyche, see John B. Cobb, Jr., *The Structure of Christian Existence* (Philadelphia: Westminster Press, 1967).

CHAPTER 6. THE COMMUNITY RESPONDS TO WOMEN

1. "Trahey, Abzug, Friedan Speak Here for UN International Women's Year," *Mundelein Today, Alumnae Line*, Chicago, vol. 1, no. 3, February, 1975, p. 1.

CHAPTER 7. WOMEN IN MINISTRY

1. Stendahl, op. cit.
2. Scanzoni and Hardesty, op. cit., p. 176.

CHAPTER 8. CONCLUSION

1. Shea, "An Approach to Pastoral Theology," p. 21.

DATE DUE

GAYLORD			PRINTED IN U.S.A.